Simon Jenkins and Anne Sloman

WITH RESPECT, AMBASSADOR

An inquiry into the Foreign Office

British Broadcasting Corporation

Published by the British Broadcasting Corporation,
35 Marylebone High Street, London W1M 4AA

ISBN 0 563 20329 3 Hardback
ISBN 0 563 20330 7 Paperback
First published 1985
© The contributors and the British Broadcasting Corporation 1985

Set in 10/12 Linotron Palatino by Input Typesetting Limited
and printed in England by Mackays of Chatham Ltd, Kent
Cover/jacket printed by George Over Limited, Rugby, Warwickshire

Contents

Foreword

This book is based on material that was gathered for a series of radio programmes, of the same name, which were first broadcast on Radio Four on 4, 11, 18, 25 March and 1 April 1984.

It follows two similar BBC series in which serving civil servants created a precedent by talking frankly on the record about their role in government and the realities behind the textbook definition of their relationship with ministers: *No, Minister*[1] about the home civil service, and *But, Chancellor*[2] about the Treasury. The Foreign Office, aware of its unpopularity in Whitehall and vilified by the popular right-wing press for its 'wetness', was eager, if a little nervous, about taking its turn at the microphone. The previous series had been thought to give participants a fair deal. The opportunity offered to the Foreign Office to answer some of its critics was felt to be helpful, despite our choice of title, which led to squeals of anguish. The choice is owed to a senior diplomat, who subsequently suffered a certain amount of ribbing from his colleagues for his disrespectful suggestion. The Foreign Secretary, Sir Geoffrey Howe, offered an alternative, arising out of a recent visit to Cairo when, on sinking into the back of the ambassador's Rolls-Royce, he was asked by the security man in the front seat, 'Which palace, Sir?' Yet the phrase 'with respect', meaning quite the opposite, echoed round so many of the ministerial and ambassadorial meetings we attended that it finally won the day.

The 'ground rules' for the recordings were the same as those which had been established in the previous two series, and are set out in full in correspondence with Lord Bancroft, then head of the home civil service, published in the preface to *No, Minister*.[3] In essence they consisted of an agreement that if officials were dissatisfied with an answer they had given they could ask for the question to be put again, and only the second answer would be used; and that up to the time the interview was concluded and we had left the room they could ask for

---

[1] *No, Minister* by Hugo Young and Anne Sloman (BBC Publications, 1982).
[2] *But, Chancellor* by Hugo Young and Anne Sloman (BBC Publications, 1983).
[3] Pages 8–12.

something they had said to be omitted, but that after that point the BBC retained sole rights over the use of the material, and the freedom to edit it as we saw fit. This agreement, though helpful in reassuring officials that they wouldn't be trapped into saying something foolish, was rarely invoked. Initially the Foreign Office was concerned to take its own recordings of the interviews, so that should a dispute arise later about an official's remarks being taken out of context they would have an independent record of what had been said. We had no objection to this in principle. Some politicians have been doing it for years – Mr Tony Benn must have a vast tape library of his interviews by journalists. In practice, having diplomats fumbling with amateur cassette machines proved an inhibiting distraction. Good interviews can only be produced from relaxed interviewees. If they felt devices for self-protection were necessary because their masters in London feared we might pull a fast one on them, interviewees would sound stilted, overcautious and unoriginal. The news department took the point, and the cassette recorders soon went back into the cupboard.

More important than the ground rules in determining the nature of the material we obtained was the decision as to where to go. We discussed the possibilities at some length with the Foreign Office, but the final itinerary was entirely our own. Some visits were clearly musts: no study of the Foreign Office could be complete without visits to Washington and Brussels. We wanted to take in a European capital in the EEC, and one outside it. Copenhagen and Stockholm were a convenient pair. An Eastern bloc country was essential too; we settled on Hungary, partly because visas presented no problem, partly because the Ambassador was willing, unlike some of his colleagues in similar posts, to risk our presence and our questions. The third world was more difficult. We were circumscribed by the cost of air fares, by time, and by the difficulty as working journalists of getting visas for many countries. In the end we decided to travel East, which enabled us to take in Beirut (the airport closed the day after we left) and Abu Dhabi, en route to New Delhi, Calcutta, Rangoon and Colombo. Calcutta, Beirut and Rangoon count as hardship posts; even so the Foreign Office felt, with some justification, that we hadn't taken in enough rough with the smooth. Both of us, it should be added, have long experience of British embassies and their staffs in countries other than those visited for this project.

Our travels were spread over a period of several months, interspersed between other commitments, and we spent between two and five days in most posts. Everywhere we went, embassies were hospitable and helpful. We sat in on immigration interviews in Delhi, a working dinner for visiting ministers in Washington, an internal meeting of the personnel department in London. We attended daily or weekly meetings at every embassy we visited. We were the guests at numerous diplomatic social occasions.

It was naturally easier to become absorbed into the daily life of the smaller missions than it was into the Foreign Office in Whitehall. It was also noticeable that the further we got from London the more relaxed our interviewees were. We collected 107 interviews, the majority, seventy-eight, with serving officials and their wives. We did talk to Foreign Office ministers past and present, to three recently retired senior diplomats, and to a number of distinguished foreign observers, but the main value of the inquiry lies in the evidence of those we were investigating. The result is presented as a snapshot of the way the Foreign Office saw itself in the six months between October 1983 and March 1984. It was not intended as a complete portrait. Hence our concentration on senior diplomats rather than their support staff, important though we know these to be to the work of the department, especially overseas.

Inevitably, our selection of material for five half-hour programmes had to be ruthless. Turning the transcripts into print has given us the opportunity to include a great deal that was excluded from the broadcasts. Some rearrangement of the material has been inevitable as a consequence, but each chapter covers the same ground as the programme on which it is based, although in some places we have clarified or reinforced our earlier conclusions. The participants are described as holding the jobs they had at the time of the broadcasts, although, as the biographies on pages 11–21 show, many of them have moved on in the intervening year.

Understandably, the radio series attracted considerable attention and comment from Whitehall and the Foreign Office itself. On the whole this was favourable, with critics who felt we had been too hard on Britain's diplomats roughly balancing those who felt we had been too timid. As we often point out, the Foreign Office is not a popular institution among public servants generally: whether fairly or unfairly we leave for readers to judge. Diplomats themselves feel this hostility and many reacted with great sensitivity to questioning which even hinted at it. Nonetheless, no discussion of the future either of the Foreign Office or of the diplomatic profession can ignore this issue of image and the political effectiveness, or ineffectiveness, which can flow from it. We respond to this and other reactions to the series in our concluding chapter.

Having decided to put themselves in our hands, the Foreign Office co-operated generously. For this we are grateful to Sir Geoffrey Howe, to his Permanent Secretary, Sir Antony Acland, to the head of the News Department, John Goulden, who (rare among press officers) was always more concerned to open doors than close them; and to his staff, particularly Richard Clarke who was unfailingly helpful over our logistical arrangements and ever patient with our requests for information.

Within the BBC we would like to thank the Controller of Radio Four, David Hatch, and the Editor of News and Current Affairs Radio, John Wilson, for giving us the opportunity (and the money) to make the original series; Judith Hocking who juggled with airline schedules, visa application forms and much else besides to make it all happen; Rosemary Edgerley for her indefatigable research assistance; and Caralyn Jacob for her additional research and for processing our words so efficiently.

Simon Jenkins
Anne Sloman
October 1984

The Participants

Acland, Sir Antony
b. 1930. *Educ.* Eton; Oxford. Entered Foreign Office 1953;
Assistant Private Secretary to Secretary of State 1959; Head of
Chancery, UK Mission, Geneva 1966–8; Counsellor and Head
of Arabian Department 1970–2; Principal Private Secretary to
Secretary of State 1972–5; Ambassador to Luxembourg 1975–7;
to Spain 1977–9; Deputy Under-Secretary of State 1980–2;
Permanent Under-Secretary of State and Head of Diplomatic
Service 1982– .

Appleyard, Len
b. 1938. *Educ.* Read School, Yorkshire; Cambridge. Entered
Foreign Office 1962; Second Secretary, Peking 1966; Second later
First Secretary, FCO 1969; First Secretary, Delhi 1971; First
Secretary (Commercial), Moscow 1975; on loan to Treasury 1978;
Counsellor (Financial), Paris 1979–82; Head of Economic
Relations Department, FCO 1982–4; Private Secretary to
Secretary of State, 1984– .

Braithwaite, Rodric
b. 1932. *Educ.* Bedales School; Cambridge. Entered Foreign
Office 1955; Head of European Integration Department
(External) 1973–5; Head of Chancery, UK Permanent Representative to EEC, Brussels 1975–8; Head of Planning Staff, FCO
1979–80; Assistant Under-Secretary of State 1980–2; Minister
(Commercial), Washington, 1982–4; Under-Secretary (Economic), FCO 1984– .

Brenton, Tony
b. 1950. *Educ.* Peter Symonds, Winchester; Cambridge. Entered
FCO 1975; First Secretary, Cairo 1978; Presidency Liaison
Officer, Brussels 1982; European Community Department
(External) FCO 1982– .

Brown, Sue
b. 1945. *Educ.* Oxford and Toronto Universities. Entered
Ministry of Agriculture, Fisheries and Food 1971; seconded to
FCO as Second later First Secretary (Agriculture), UK Permanent Representative to the EEC, Brussels 1974–7; First Secretary

11

(Agriculture), Washington 1982– .

Brzezinski, Zbigniew
b. 1928. *Educ.* McGill and Harvard Universities. Professor of Public Law and Government, Columbia University 1962– ; Member of Policy Planning Council, Department of State 1966–8; Special White House Assistant for National Security 1977–81.

Bullard, Sir Julian
b. 1928. *Educ.* Rugby; Oxford. Entered Diplomatic Service 1953; Political Agent, Dubai 1968; Head of Eastern European and Soviet Department 1971; Minister, Bonn 1975; Deputy Under-Secretary of State 1979; Deputy to Permanent Under-Secretary of State 1982–4; Ambassador to West Germany 1984– .

Butler, Sir Michael
b. 1927. *Educ.* Winchester; Oxford. Entered Foreign Office 1950; Counsellor, Washington 1971–2; Head of European Integration Department, FCO 1972–4; Assistant Under-Secretary in charge of European Community Affairs, 1974–6; Deputy Under-Secretary of State 1976–9; Ambassador and Permanent UK Representative to the EEC, Brussels 1979– .

Cahn, Andrew
b. 1951. *Educ.* Bedales; Cambridge. Entered Ministry of Agriculture, Fisheries and Food 1973; First Secretary, UKREP Brussels 1982– .

Chaplin, Edward
b. 1951. *Educ.* Wellington; Cambridge. Entered Foreign Office 1973; Second Secretary, Brussels 1977; First Secretary, Near East and North Africa Desk, FCO 1981– .

Davies, Derek
b. 1933. *Educ.* Paget's School; Birmingham College of Advanced Technology. Chief Engineer, GEC Pakistan 1958–62; Director, GEC Electrical Projects Ltd and Howgec Nigeria Ltd 1979; Chairman of UK Airports Group 1981– .

Davignon, Viscount Etienne
b. 1932. *Educ.* University of Louvain. Head of Office of Minister of Foreign Affairs, Belgium 1963; Political Director, Ministry for Foreign Affairs, Belgium 1969; Member (with responsibility for industrial affairs) 1977–84; and Vice-President 1981–4,

Commission of the European Communities.

Dunstone, Denis
b. 1935. *Educ.* St John's School, Abergavenny; Epsom College; Cambridge. Joined British Petroleum 1959; Manager, Marine Sales, BP London 1978–81; Managing Director, BP Denmark 1981– .

Fenn, Nicholas
b. 1936. *Educ.* Kingswood; Cambridge. Entered Foreign Office 1959; Third later Second Secretary, Rangoon 1959–63; Assistant Private Secretary to Secretary of State 1964; Deputy Head, Energy Department, FCO 1972–5; Counsellor, Head of Chancery and Consul General, Peking 1975–7; Head of News Department, FCO 1979–82; Ambassador to Burma 1982– .

Fisher, George
b. 1930. *Educ.* Rhymney Grammar School; University College, Cardiff; Institute of Education, London University. Joined British Council 1959; Cultural Attaché and British Council Representative, Hungary 1980–4.

Fortescue, John Adrian
b. 1941. *Educ.* Uppingham; Cambridge; London School of Economics. Private Secretary to Ambassador, Paris 1968; First Secretary, UKDEL Brussels 1972; on loan to Commission of European Communities, Brussels 1973; Counsellor, Head of Presidency Unit, European Community Department (External); FCO 1981; Head of Chancery, Budapest 1983–4; European Commission, 1984– .

Gergen, David
b. 1942. *Educ.* Yale; Harvard. Staff Assistant, Nixon Administration, Washington 1971–2; Special Counsel to President Ford, Director, White House Office Communications, Washington 1975–7; Resident Fellow American Enterprise Institute, Assistant to President for communications 1981–4; Fellow of Institute of Politics, Harvard 1984 and Visiting Fellow in Communications, AEI 1984– .

Gore-Booth, David
b. 1943. *Educ.* Eton; Oxford. Entered Foreign Office 1964; First Secretary, UKREP Brussels 1974; Assistant Head of Financial Relations Department, FCO 1978; Counsellor (Economic/ Commercial), Jedda 1980–3; Head of Chancery, UK Mission to the UN, New York 1983– .

Gore-Booth, Mary
b. 1949. Married David Gore-Booth 1977. Freelance interpreter and translator.

Gray, Cyril
b. 1934. *Educ.* Armagh Technical School; Portadown Technical School. Entered FCO on loan from Northern Ireland Office 1980; First Secretary, Washington 1980–4; Industrial Development Board, Northern Ireland 1984– .

Hannay, David
b. 1935. *Educ.* Winchester; Oxford. Entered FCO 1959; Second later First Secretary, UK Delegation to European Communities, Brussels 1965–70; First Secretary, UK Negotiating Team with European Communities, Brussels 1970–2; Chef de Cabinet to Sir Christopher Soames, Vice-President of EEC 1973–7; Head of Energy, Science and Space Department, FCO 1977–9; Head of Middle East Department, FCO 1979; Assistant Under-Secretary of State, European Integration 1979–84; Minister, Washington 1984– .

Harding, Roger
b. 1935. *Educ.* Price's School, Fareham; Southern Grammar School, Portsmouth. Hampshire Board of Trade 1954–74; entered Ministry of Defence 1974; Head of Defence Secretariat 8 1979–82; Counsellor, Defence Supply, British Embassy, Washington 1982– .

Harris, Tom
b. 1945. *Educ.* Mercers' School, London; Haberdashers'; Cambridge. Board of Trade 1966–9; FCO 1969–71; Department of Trade and Industry, Private Secretary to Minister of Aerospace 1971–2; on loan to Cabinet Office 1976–8; Private Secretary to Secretary of State for Trade 1978–9; Commercial Counsellor, Washington, on loan to FCO 1983– .

Hayday, Anthony
b. 1930. *Educ.* Beckenham and Penge Grammar School. Entered Diplomatic Service 1950; First Secretary, New Delhi 1969; Head of Chancery, Freetown 1973; First Secretary on loan to Commonwealth Secretariat 1976–80; Deputy High Commissioner, Calcutta 1981– .

Henderson, Sir Nicholas
b. 1919. *Educ.* Stowe; Oxford. Entered Diplomatic Service 1942;

Minister of State's Office, Cairo, 1942–3; Assistant Private Secretary to the Foreign Secretary 1944–7; Head of Northern Department, FO 1963; Private Secretary to Foreign Secretary 1963–5; Minister, Madrid 1965–9; Ambassador to Poland 1969–72; to West Germany 1972–5; to France 1975–9; to United States 1979–82.

Howe, Rt Hon. Sir Geoffrey
b. 1926. *Educ.* Winchester; Cambridge. Conservative MP 1964–6; 1970– . Solicitor-General 1970–2; Minister for Trade and Consumer Affairs 1972–4; Chancellor of the Exchequer 1979–83; Foreign Secretary 1983– .

Huxley, Roger
b. 1939. *Educ.* Leamington College. Entered FCO E-stream 1970; Jakarta 1973; Athens 1977; Second Secretary (Commercial), Abu Dhabi 1980–4; FCO 1984– .

Jackson, Michael
b. 1940. *Educ.* Queen Elizabeth School, Darlington; Paisley Grammar School; Glasgow University. Scottish Office 1961–70; seconded to Ministry of Agriculture, Fisheries and Food 1971–2; seconded to FCO and served in The Hague 1973–4. Transferred to Diplomatic Service 1974; Counsellor (Commercial) Buenos Aires 1981–2; FCO (Falklands Islands Department) 1982; Head of Chancery, Stockholm, 1982– .

Jones-Parry, Emyr
b. 1947. *Educ.* University College, Cardiff; Cambridge. Entered FCO 1973; First Secretary (Energy), UKREP Brussels 1982– .

Kirkpatrick, Jeanne
b. 1926. *Educ.* Stephens College; Columbia University; University of Paris. Professor of Government, Georgetown University 1978–80; Resident Scholar, American Enterprise Institute 1977–80; US Ambassador to United Nations 1981–4.

Lambert, David
b. 1941. *Educ.* Bancrofts School, Woodford Green. Board of Trade 1959–69; entered FCO E-stream 1969; Kuwait 1970; Lagos 1973; Khartoum 1974; FCO 1977–80; Paris 1980; FCO 1982–3; First Secretary, Copenhagen 1983– .

Luers, William
b. 1929. *Educ.* Hamilton College; Columbia University. Second

Secretary, American Embassy, Moscow 1963–5; Political Counsellor, American Embassy, Caracas 1969–73; Deputy Executive Secretary, Department of State 1973–5; US Ambassador to Venezuela 1978–83; US Ambassador to Czechoslovakia 1983–   .

Maguire, Gerry
b. 1944. Home Office 1964–   . Open University degree 1978; Immigration Officer, New Delhi 1979–   .

Marsden, William
b. 1940. *Educ.* Winchester; Lawrenceville School, USA; Cambridge; London. Entered Foreign Office 1962; Private Secretary to Ambassador, Rome 1966; Second Secretary (Commercial), Rome 1967; First Secretary, FCO 1971; Cultural Attaché, Moscow 1976–9; Assistant Head, European Community Department FCO 1979–81; Counsellor, UKREP Brussels 1981–   .

Mellon, James
b. 1929. *Educ.* St Aloysius College; Glasgow University. Department of Agriculture for Scotland 1953–60; Agricultural Attaché, Copenhagen and The Hague 1960–3; entered Foreign Office 1963; Counsellor (Commercial), East Berlin 1975–6; Head of Trade Relations and Export Department, FCO 1976–8; High Commissioner in Ghana and Ambassador to Togo 1978–83; Ambassador to Denmark 1983–   .

Miers, David
b. 1937. *Educ.* Winchester; Oxford. Entered Foreign Office 1963; Private Secretary to Minister of State 1968; to Parliamentary Under-Secretary of State 1969–70; Counsellor and Head of Chancery, Tehran 1977–80; Head of Middle East Department, FCO 1980–3; Ambassador to Lebanon 1983–   .

Mooncie, Linda
Married Alan Mooncie, now Commercial Attaché, Stockholm, 1969.

Murray, Sir Donald
b. 1924. *Educ.* Canterbury School; Oxford. Entered Diplomatic Service 1948; First Secretary (Commercial) Stockholm 1958; Head of Chancery, Saigon 1952; Counsellor 1965; Head of South East Asia Department 1966; Counsellor, Tehran 1969–72; Royal College of Defence Studies 1973; Ambassador to Libya 1974–6; Assistant Under-Secretary of State 1977–80; Ambassador to

Sweden 1980–4.

Nicholas, Sir John
b. 1924. *Educ.* Holly Lodge Grammar School; Birmingham University. Entered War Office 1949. Transferred to Commonwealth Relations Office 1957; Diplomatic Service Inspector 1967–9; Deputy High Commissioner and Counsellor (Commercial), Colombo 1970–1; Deputy High Commissioner, Calcutta 1974–6; Consul General, Melbourne 1976; High Commissioner to Sri Lanka and Ambassador to Republic of Maldives 1979– .

Otunnu, Olara
b. 1950. *Educ.* Kampala; Oxford. Delegate to National Consultative Council, Kampala 1979–80; Ugandan Permanent Representative to the United Nations 1981– .

Owen, Rt Hon. Dr David
b. 1938. *Educ.* Bradfield College; Cambridge. Labour MP 1966–81, SDP 1981– . Parliamentary Under-Secretary of State for Defence 1968–70, for DHSS 1974; Minister of State DHSS 1974–6, FCO 1976–7; Foreign Secretary 1977–9; Co-founder SDP 1981; Leader, SDP 1983– .

Palliser, Sir Michael
b. 1922. *Educ.* Wellington College; Oxford. Entered Diplomatic Service 1947; Private Secretary to Permanent Under-Secretary 1954–6; Counsellor and seconded to Imperial Defence College 1963; Head of Planning Staff 1964; a Private Secretary to the Prime Minister 1966; Minister, Paris 1969; Ambassador and UK Permanent Representative to European Communities, Brussels 1973–5; Permanent Under-Secretary of State and Head of Diplomatic Service 1975–82.

Parsons, Sir Anthony
b. 1922. *Educ.* Kings School, Canterbury; Oxford. Entered Foreign Office 1954; Political Agent, Bahrain 1965–9; Counsellor, UK Mission to UN, New York 1969–71; Under-Secretary FCO 1971–4; Ambassador to Iran 1974–9; UK Permanent Representative to UN 1979–82; Special Adviser to the Prime Minister on foreign affairs 1982–3.

Pooley, Peter
b. 1936. *Educ.* Brentwood; Cambridge. Entered Ministry of Agriculture, Fisheries and Food 1959; seconded to Diplomatic Service, Brussels 1961–3; Minister (Agriculture), UKREP, Brus-

sels 1979–82; Deputy Director General (Agriculture), European Commission 1983– .

Rainbow, Basil
b. 1931. *Educ.* Palatine School, Blackpool. Entered Diplomatic Service 1949; Vice-Consul, Osaka 1975; Second Secretary (Consular/Administration), Calcutta 1982– .

Reid, Gordon
b. 1956. *Educ.* Fortrose Academy; Borough Muir School; Polytechnic of Central London. Entered FCO 1980; Second Secretary, Budapest 1982– .

Renwick, Robin
b. 1937. *Educ.* St Paul's; Cambridge. Entered Foreign Office 1963; Private Secretary to Minister of State 1970–2; First Secretary, Paris 1972–6; Counsellor, Cabinet Office 1976; Head of Rhodesia Department, FCO 1978–80; Head of Chancery, Washington 1981–4; Assistant Under-Secretary of State, European Community 1984– .

Rifkind, Malcolm
b. 1946. *Educ.* George Watson's College; Edinburgh University. Conservative MP 1974– ; Parliamentary Under-Secretary of State, Scottish Office 1979–82; FCO 1982–3; Minister of State FCO 1983– .

Rowlands, Ted
b. 1940. *Educ.* Rhondda and Wirral Grammar Schools; London University. Labour MP 1966–70, 72– ; Parliamentary Under-Secretary of State, Welsh Office 1969–70, 74–5; FCO 1975–6; Minister of State, FCO 1976–9.

Smallman, David
b. 1940. National Assistance Board 1961; Commonwealth Office 1966; Islamabad 1967; Second Secretary, Nicosia 1971; Second Secretary (Commercial), Singapore 1973; First Secretary, FCO 1977; Consul, Aden 1981; First Secretary and Head of Chancery, Rangoon 1983– .

Solesby, Tessa
b. 1932. *Educ.* Clifton High School; Oxford. Ministry of Labour and National Service 1954–5; entered Foreign Office 1956; First Secretary, UK Mission New York 1970–2; Counsellor 1975; on secondment to NATO international staff, Brussels 1975–8; Counsellor, East Berlin 1978–81; Head of Central Africa Department, FCO 1982– .

Sullivan, Kim
b. 1949. *Educ.* Minehead; Oxford. Third later Second Secretary, FCO 1974; Language student Cambridge and Hong Kong 1975–6; Second later First Secretary, Peking 1977; on loan to Cabinet Office 1980–2; First Secretary (Commercial), Stockholm 1982– .

Thomas, Derek
b. 1929. *Educ.* Radley College; Cambridge. Entered Foreign Office 1953; UK Delegation to Brussels Conference 1961–2; First Secretary, FO 1962; seconded to Treasury 1969–70; Financial Counsellor, Paris 1971–5; Assistant Under-Secretary of State (Economic) 1976–9; Minister (Commercial) later Minister, Washington 1979–84; Deputy Under-Secretary of State (Europe) and Political Director 1984– .

Unwin, Peter
b. 1932. *Educ.* Ampleforth; Oxford. Entered Foreign Office 1956; on loan to Bank of England 1973; Counsellor (Economic), Bonn 1973–6; Head of Personnel Policy Department, FCO 1976–9; Sabbatical Harvard University, 1979–80; Minister (Economic), Bonn 1980–3; Ambassador to Hungary 1983– .

Urquhart, Brian
b. 1919. *Educ.* Westminster; Oxford. Personal Assistant to Trygve Lie, First Secretary-General of UN 1946–9; UN Representative, Congo 1961–2; Assistant Secretary-General, UN 1972–4; Under-Secretary-General, UN 1974– .

Wade-Gery, Sir Robert
b. 1929. *Educ.* Winchester; Oxford. Entered Diplomatic Service 1951; Private Secretary to Permanent Under-Secretary, later Southern Department 1957–60; First Secretary, Tel Aviv 1960–4; Foreign Office (Planning) 1964–7; First Secretary, Saigon 1977–8; First Secretary, later Counsellor, Cabinet Office (on secondment as Secretary to Duncan Report) 1968; on loan to Bank of England 1969; Head of Financial Policy and Aid Department 1969–70; on loan to Cabinet Office (Central Policy Review Staff) 1971–3; Minister, Madrid 1973–7; Minister, Moscow 1977–9; Deputy Secretary of the Cabinet 1979–82; High Commissioner to India 1982– .

Wade-Gery, Lady Sarah
Married Robert Wade-Gery 1962.

Walker, Harold (Hookey)
b. 1932. *Educ.* Winchester; Oxford. Entered Foreign Office 1955; Middle East Centre for Arab Studies 1957; Assistant Political Agent, Dubai 1958; Private Secretary to Parliamentary Under-Secretary 1962–3; Principal Instructor MECAS 1963; First Secretary (Commercial), Washington 1970; Counsellor, Jedda 1973; Deputy Head, later Head Personnel Operations Department 1975–6; Ambassador and Consul General to Bahrain 1979–81; Ambassador to United Arab Emirates 1981–   .

Walsh, Harry
b. 1939. *Educ.* Westhill High School, Montreal; McGill University; Cambridge. Entered HM Treasury 1966; Private Secretary to Chancellor of Duchy of Lancaster 1974–6; Cabinet Office Secretariat 1978–80; Counsellor (Economic), Washington 1980–   .

Williamson, David
b. 1934. *Educ.* Tonbridge School; Exeter. Entered Ministry of Agriculture, Fisheries and Food 1958; Principal Private Secretary to successive Ministers of Agriculture 1967–70; Milk Products Division, Marketing Policy Division and Food Policy Division 1970–4; Under-Secretary-General Agricultural Policy Group, EEC Group 1974–7; Deputy Director General (Agriculture), European Commission 1977–83; Deputy Secretary, Cabinet Office 1983–   .

Wood, Andrew
b. 1940. *Educ.* Ardingly; Cambridge. Entered Foreign Office 1961; seconded to Cabinet Office 1971; First Secretary, FCO 1973; Counsellor, Belgrade 1976; Head of Chancery, Moscow 1979; Head of West European Department, FCO 1982; Head of Personnel Department, FCO 1983–   .

Wright, Lady Lillian
Married Oliver Wright 1942.

Wright, Sir Oliver
b. 1921. *Educ.* Solihull School; Cambridge. Entered Diplomatic Service 1945; Private Secretary to Foreign Secretary 1960–4; Private Secretary to Prime Minister 1964–6; Ambassador to Denmark 1966–9; seconded to Home Office as UK Representative to Northern Ireland Government 1969–70; Chief Clerk, Diplomatic Service 1970–2; Deputy Under-Secretary of State,

1972–5; Ambassador to West Germany 1975–81; Director, Siemens Ltd, 1981–2; Ambassador to United States 1982–   .

Young, Rt Hon. Baroness Janet
b. 1926; *Educ.* Dragon School, Oxford; Headington School; Oxford. Baroness in Waiting (Government Whip) 1972–3; Parliamentary Under-Secretary of State, Department of the Environment 1973–4; Minister of State, Department of Education and Science 1979–81; Chancellor, Duchy of Lancaster 1981–2; Leader of House of Lords 1981–3; Lord Privy Seal 1982–3; Minister of State, FCO 1983–   .

The Chosen Ones

The British diplomat is a civil servant apart. He lives, works and entertains in surroundings which bespeak a grander age than ours, a world of protocols and butlers, memoranda and Daimlers, his Frenchified vocabulary studded with *aides-mémoire*, *placements* and *corps d'élite*. He is a far cry from the bureaucrat of popular caricature, with his shiny trousers, chipped tea-cup and the 6.30 home to Sidcup. Loyal servant of the Crown he may be, but as member of an antique and mysterious freemasonry.

Diplomacy has claim to be regarded as genuinely the 'oldest profession'. Harold Nicolson, the Boswell of the profession, traced its history back to Homer's heralds, in line of descent from the messenger gods themselves.[1] As soon as men began to combine, and thus to fight, envoys had to carry with them the trust of their communities. They were custodians of information. They were given power to make decisions on the basis of that information, decisions ultimately of war and peace. They had to be granted absolute protection or the relations between states would break down. They became the symbol of international order, one of the world's great professional societies, a natural élite.

Since the Second World War, this professionalism has been under attack. Its British citadel, the Foreign Office, seems to many to epitomise all that is most closed and old-fashioned in public administration. International communication has become easier. Technology has eliminated the need for much traditional diplomatic formalism. Defence and trade, tourism and culture, finance and multinational industry have all established new conduits for relations between states, quite outside the ambassadorial circuit. At the same time, the growth in the number of sovereign states and the immature character of their leaderships have often snapped the fine thread of diplomatic custom and practice and brought it into disrepute.

Many diplomats both in Britain and abroad have become defensive, even doubtful of their role. Getting them to express

---

[1] Harold Nicolson, *Diplomacy* (Butterworth, London, 1939), p. 19.

these doubts on the record is not easy. If journalism is the art
of clarification, diplomacy is often that of genteel obfuscation.
Diplomats are intuitively averse to discussing their profession
in public (often flatly contradicting what they say with some
passion in private). Yet most of them complain of being misun-
derstood. All British civil servants have felt themselves politically alienated since Mrs Thatcher's aggressively anti-public
sector government came to power. Diplomats feel this particularly – perhaps because in the past they have felt a professional
affinity for conservatism.

Diplomats are angered – in some cases to the point of despair
– at the public attention focused on the paraphernalia of diplomacy rather than its substance. They regard the paraphernalia,
the entertaining, the fine buildings, the allowances, the
protocol, as essential to the substance. Yet the substance, the
maintenance of international peace and order and the
promotion of Britain's interests abroad, appears to have gone
by default. Diplomats know that in recent years they have lost
status and influence to other departments in Whitehall.
Younger ones see the need for an urgent redefinition of their
profession in terms compatible with modern technology and
world politics. Others long for the leaders of their profession
merely to assert more forcibly diplomacy's traditional verities.
It is a desire for intellectual leadership both groups share with
diplomats in Europe and America.

Although the popular image of the diplomatic profession
may, to diplomats, be one of irritating caricature, it is not easy to
get them to define their professional objectives. Most, however,
would probably take their lead from the idealism of the head of
the Diplomatic Service and Permanent Secretary to the Foreign
Office, Sir Antony Acland:

Acland:

I think that most of us would like to see the world made a
safer place. We all perhaps have an ambition to make our
contribution to the settlement of a major issue in dispute,
whether it is in the Middle East or problems over our
remaining dependent territories or the whole question of
arms control. When, to my surprise, I was appointed Permanent Under-Secretary to the Foreign Office, I was asked
what I would most like to see achieved during my period in
that job. I said, without really any hesitation, that I would
like to see a significant, conclusive, balanced, verifiable and

effective measure of arms control. It would release resources for more productive activities and would enable people in Britain and around the world to sleep more peacefully in their beds.

A much younger diplomat, William Marsden, with the British delegation to the EEC in Brussels, defined the profession in very similar terms:

Marsden:

The world is a dangerous place and it is essential that the positions of governments who determine whether there is peace or war – and whether Britain gets a decent deal in the world – are clearly understood and clearly put forward. The basic *raison d'être* of diplomats is to do that. A world without people who articulated it carefully would be a very dangerous one.

Through it all, the diplomat retains his sense of being a special sort of public servant. Sir Julian Bullard, deputy to the Permanent Secretary and Political Director of the Foreign Office, is one of British diplomacy's most senior figures. He describes briskly his view of the modern Diplomatic Service:

Bullard:

I suppose we are an institution apart. We are one per cent of the civil service as a whole. I don't shun the word élite. I don't know when the word élite began to go downhill. *Corps d'élite* used to be a body that you would give your eye-teeth to get into. I think it was that when I joined the Foreign Service, as it was then called. And indeed I think it must still be that, judging by the number and the quality of the people we have applying to get into the Service.

The institution to which Sir Julian refers is indeed small. Despite having embraced the former Colonial and Commonwealth Offices in the 1960s, the officially titled Foreign and Commonwealth Office is one of the smallest departments of state. At the last count it was just 6527 strong, twenty per cent down over the past two decades. Of these, less than 3000 are career diplomats in 'administrative' grades. With this establishment, the department must staff 213 posts covering 164 countries abroad, as well as maintaining a foreign-policy function in Whitehall.

The men and women who staff the Foreign Office are undoubtedly the pick of the annual civil service intake. Although previously the Diplomatic Service had its own private selection procedure, its recruits now come to it through the civil service selection board, but with the Foreign Office making its final choice from those who achieve the top 'A' rating and who have expressed a preference for it. This has undoubtedly had an effect in broadening the social and educational background of its intake, though it is still disproportionately weighted towards public schools (50%) and Oxbridge (59%).

It is also overwhelmingly male. The marriage bar which forced women diplomats to leave the Service when they married was lifted only in 1972 and the few women who occupy senior diplomatic posts are all unmarried.[1] Two years ago only eleven per cent of the administrative trainee intake in the Foreign Office were women. Now the proportion is twenty-five per cent, but unsurprisingly there are only two 'dependent' husbands at first secretary level, and none above. In the Diplomatic Service, when they talk of spouses they still almost always mean wives.

That said, a profession with such panglossian objectives remains a curious choice for a modern undergraduate. So what motivated those who are now progressing up the Service? Sir Robert Wade-Gery, High Commissioner in New Delhi, went to Winchester and then to New College and All Souls, Oxford. He readily admits to the part popular image played in his choice of career in 1951:

Wade-Gery:

It was a fashionable thing to try to do when I was at university. I thought it sounded like a nice easy life being paid to go to cocktail parties. I think, to be a shade less flip, I did have some idea when thinking about it at Oxford that the interest factor would be very high. I remember feeling that post-war Britain was a fairly small and parochial place, and that a profession that involved one in spending one's time thinking about the wider world would have a kind of perennial interest, and I think it has turned out that way.

David Gore-Booth is a decade younger than Sir Robert; he is now Head of Chancery of our delegation to the United Nations in New York. Like many diplomats, he entered the Service because he had been brought up in it. His father, later Perma-

---

[1] Dame Anne Warburton, Britain's only woman ambassador, heads the UK delegation to the United Nations in Geneva. Patricia Hutchinson, formerly ambassador to Uruguay, is consul-general in Barcelona.

nent Secretary at the Foreign Office, lived in the same house in New Delhi now occupied by the Wade-Gerys.[1] (The Gore-Booths' 'nursery bearer' is still on the embassy books.) His reason for entering the profession of diplomat seemed to him as inevitable as service overseas might have been to a young man in the nineteenth century:

Gore-Booth:

I suppose the obvious answer is that my father was one. Secondly, I had an arts education, which didn't therefore fit me for computers or whatever was the then equivalent. Also, I dare say a sense of the romantic had something to do with it. I am ambitious, I like being promoted, not least for the money. I haven't set my heart on any post, whether terminal or on the way, and I don't necessarily aim to do the things my father did, though in a romantic sort of way it might be quite nice to end up as he did at the top of the shop. But I'm not setting myself that target. As long as I go upwards and to interesting posts, preferably both those things, I shall be happy. I hope I shall end up as an ambassador somewhere along the line, but of course that's for others, rather than myself, to decide.

The Foreign Office is keen to parade those younger recruits drawn from what it discreetly terms a 'wider background'. Gordon Reid, on his first posting as second secretary in Budapest, is one such: a Scotsman educated at state schools who took a degree in languages at the Polytechnic of Central London. Yet even he finds it hard to explain his ambition in markedly different terms from those of his elders:

Reid:

I suppose I could start with the simplistic things which we were warned should not be our main motive in applying for the Foreign Office – 'Have languages, will travel' is one. I suppose I saw a certain glamour in the Office, but that wasn't really a major attraction. I thought the idea of going abroad and living abroad and getting to know a country well, having the time to get to know a country well, and indeed having a brief to do so, was something I wanted to do.

---

[1] Lord Gore-Booth (1909–84) was British High Commissioner in India 1960–5; Permanent Under-Secretary of State at the Foreign Office 1965–9; Head of the Diplomatic Service 1968–9.

Foreign Office selection procedure is both subtle and gruelling. Candidates spend days together, chairing mock meetings, drafting reports, making recommendations, watched all the time by personnel officers. They are also subjected to intensive interview, as much to elicit their attitude of mind as to discern any particular linguistic or other skills. Peter Unwin, now ambassador in Budapest, used to conduct such interviews. He sought answers to two questions:

Unwin:

First, 'Are you prepared to shoot from the hip?' I mean by that, are you prepared to deal in a hurry with things which you could deal with better and more happily if you had longer, but life isn't like that. Secondly, I used to ask them, 'Are you prepared to live your life on other people's terms, always interested in other people's politics, other people's society, other people's languages, other people's history?' If you are not, then you are not well suited for the Diplomatic Service.

The new recruit finds him or herself tossed into an environment which many find confusing and rather amateur. The first skill which the Foreign Office demands of its novices is linguistic, roughly half going off for at least six months to study a difficult language. Apart from French and another European language, most diplomats will sooner or later be expected to master at least one difficult tongue. This will in most cases dictate much of their overseas career, and almost certainly their first ambassadorial posting.

Before the dissolution of empire, the major non-European sphere of British diplomatic activity was the Middle East. The Foreign Office had its own Arabic language school, known as MECAS, in the hills behind Beirut and its alumni were regarded as a special élite. Those days are over. Other languages – Russian, Japanese, Chinese – are now as much in demand as Arabic, and MECAS has been overwhelmed by the Lebanese civil war.[1] It has taken with it many a Foreign Office memory of warm Levantine nights and dreams of glory in the capitals of Arabia. Yet hard languages are still a Foreign Office

---

[1] MECAS (Middle East Centre for Arab Studies) was established in Jerusalem in 1943 under the aegis of British Military Command in the Middle East and moved to Shemlan in the Lebanon when it came under the Foreign Office in 1947. It was finally evacuated in 1978 and wound up in 1981.

speciality. While the rest of Whitehall can mug up its French or Italian for a European posting, only the Foreign Office can deliver Burmese or Hungarian or Korean on demand – to the admiration (and often puzzlement) of other foreign services which make no such demands of their members.

The languages requirement is immensely costly. It takes from six months to two years to give even the ablest linguist a worthwhile working knowledge of Arabic or Mandarin or Japanese. The language may be used for no more than six years throughout a career – and then only on occasions. Many diplomats spend much of their time monitoring the local media and interpreting, tasks which could be performed by specialised linguists, even locally engaged staff, on a more cost-effective basis. The Service nonetheless takes immense pride in its linguistic self-efficiency. James Mellon, ambassador in Copenhagen, is a fluent Danish speaker:

Mellon:

I demand that the staff here do apply themselves to the study of Danish, not just as a theoretical matter, but because it is essential for many of them to have a knowledge of Danish in order to do their job. I know that many of my Danish friends speak perfect English and they certainly speak better English than I will ever speak Danish. On the other hand, there are large areas of Danish society where, to put it mildly, it is very very useful to be able to speak and understand the language. When I came here, every member of chancery, the agricultural attaché, the counsellor, the first secretary, the third secretary, were all speaking Danish and able to do business in Danish, and I won't run this embassy on any other basis. We have to provide material for our government machine to be able to operate and one of the most effective ways of getting that material is to be able to read the papers quickly, to follow what's happening on the television news, to be able to follow the nature of debates in the *Folketing* [the Danish parliament] and to be able to communicate with people.

Apart from language training, the Foreign Office provides its recruits with little by way of induction. Diplomacy is a profession with no formal corpus of knowledge; it is learned on the job. Such ostensibly useful skills as applied economics, development theory, international law, defence studies, business management, accountancy, even journalism or public relations, have to be picked up as the recruit progresses through his career. When he first joined, David Hannay, now under-secretary for European affairs, was nonplussed by it all:

Hannay:

I was a bit shattered by the total lack of anybody telling you what you were meant to do. When I joined the Service in 1959 there was no training at all, except language training. I was sent to learn Persian, which I did on a language course at the School of Oriental and African Studies at London University, and then I went to Tehran. From there I went to Kabul in Afghanistan and that was all done very efficiently and effectively. But as to how I should do my job, or what my job consisted of, there was absolutely no training at all. It was the old British custom of throwing you in at the deep end and leaving to you to see if you could swim. It threw one a bit.

Gordon Reid had a similar experience:

Reid:

We had a so-called induction course which took a week in Palace Chambers down on the Embankment, where for example we were taught how to draft in about four hours. This, as everyone knows, is not long enough and if you haven't got what it takes you won't make it anyway. We did a language proficiency test. Having got a good degree in languages, I was hopeful that I would do well, and duly did. Our choice was between those hard languages available – Hungarian, Polish, Russian inevitably, Arabic, Chinese, in my year there was Korean. We didn't get to choose country X or language Y, but we got to express preferences.

To the Foreign Office, the essence of becoming a diplomat is learning to live abroad and operate within the conventions of an embassy. This is not just a matter of knowing the ropes of an office, knowing procedures and acquiring administrative skills. It is learning how to cope in a foreign country, not as a tourist nor as an expatriate but as a working official. This means 'getting on with foreigners' – diplomats have a fixation that this is a highly specialist skill – and also settling into an embassy's often very close collegiate atmosphere. Tessa Solesby, head of the Central Africa department at the Foreign Office, was thrown in at the deep end on her first posting in the Philippines:

Solesby:

That, I suppose, was the biggest culture shock of my career.

I'd never been outside Western Europe before and here I was in a totally different climate living in a little wooden house on stilts. I've always been terrified of anything that creeps or crawls, and it was full of things that crept and crawled. It was a Jill-of-all-trades sort of job in a tiny embassy, and I had to turn my hand to political work, to aid work and to working with trade unionists, technicians, business people. I supervised a British library that had been set up by British firms. I had my own radio broadcast every two weeks. I wrote articles for the press. The other quite extraordinary thing which I hadn't expected was that in this rather small capital I was suddenly in a small way a public figure. I was newsworthy. I'd have somebody to dinner and I'd find that somehow or other the local press had found out and there was this photographer elbowing his way through the front door with the guests. All this was completely new to me, and it taught me the first great lesson for any diplomat: you've got to be adaptable.

Most diplomats, though by no means all, will spend two-thirds of their careers abroad, with half that time in the area of their language specialisation. At home in London, the diplomat is little different from a home civil servant. He can live a normal life, commuting between home and office, and be able to keep the two reasonably distinct. Abroad, he is always on duty. He is expected to be the eyes, the ears and even the mouth of the British government and people. His family cannot avoid being part of this duty: they too are a local manifestation of British-ness. The diplomat reports back regularly to London on the events of his host country. Equally, he must keep his host nation abreast of what is happening in London. He is thus journalist, public relations man and local 'company rep' for Whitehall.

In addition, the diplomat is 'baby-sitting' for British interests. This means giving advice to struggling businessmen; bailing out tourists in trouble; running an information and cultural advice bureau; entertaining and briefing VIPs out from London; providing the local expatriate community with a patch of Britain and a gin and tonic to remind them of home. The diplomat must represent the embassy at the social and cultural functions which fill his diary and frequently drive him, and his wife, into a despair of tedium. To a considerable extent, the skills involved in this work are those of social intercourse rather than intellectual application. They require of the diplomat that he be personable, be interested in (or able to feign interest in) people, however dull, and possess an exhaustive command of smalltalk. From these skills, it is a short step to the familiar charge of 'smoothness' so often laid at the diplomat's door, of being so well-rounded he will roll wherever pushed. Peter Pooley, formerly a senior Ministry of Agriculture official, now with the Common Market Commission in Brussels, observed his Foreign Office contemporaries with the eye of an Anthony Powell:

Pooley:

It was a great shock to me as a young man when I was living with a diplomat for a while. Going to cocktail parties and dinners with him, I was sat down at the table afterwards while he got out his notebook and quizzed me. 'Who was this man? What was his exact position? Was he married to the American girl? Oh no, the American girl was married to the other chap. Have you got the spelling of his name? Where does he come from? Is he successful? Or is he not successful?' All this was going down in the notebook, so that on the next occasion, having swotted up his notebook in advance, he could say, 'Hello, George. How is Sally? How are things in steel at this moment?' This makes a very good impact initially. But when you see it done professionally and slickly, it has the reverse effect. The professional charmer is always going to meet with a certain amount of resistance, and the true professional diplomat may meet with a certain amount of resistance as well.

Diplomats naturally see these qualities differently. The British ambassador in Washington, Sir Oliver Wright, is a strong personality who, to some observers, might appear to err on the side of professional 'smoothness'. He accepts that the character of the diplomat is moulded to some extent by the nature of his work:

Wright:

You have a common operating experience and get to know each other extremely well – and you have to trust each other particularly well. So in the Diplomatic Service you do have the same sort of flavour as you might have in a regiment. You depend upon each other so much more in our sort of job than people do in ordinary life at home. You have to rub along with a lot of different sorts of foreigners. Whether this makes you urbane or whatever, I simply don't know.

31

All I know is that one develops certain techniques for living in a great number of different places in the world and with a variety of different cultures, and for this you have to have a certain adaptability and a certain facility for getting on. This does rub corners off, no doubt at all, and if your definition of someone who's had his corners rubbed off is smooth, OK, I'm with you.

Another ambassador, Peter Unwin in Budapest, has clearly pondered the question of professional style but regards it as an occupational hazard of diplomatic technique:

Unwin:

I think it can be a danger and it is something we should always watch out for. There are instances in the past where perhaps we have been too superficial. We need to know a lot, but we don't need to drown ourselves in unnecessary or irrelevant knowledge, and what can seem like the superficial skill of a smoothie can also be the skill of putting aside what is just the dross and of extracting what is essential, that leads to that crucial perception.

Given its range of tasks, the career structure of the men and women who comprise the Diplomatic Service is extraordinarily rigid. A young diplomat entering as a graduate in the top A-stream will go on his first posting as a third secretary. If considered a success he will soon rise to second secretary. He will probably be moved every two or three years from his country of language specialisation to somewhere completely different and back to a job in London. By the end of his twenties he will almost certainly be a first secretary, the junior executive grade of the Service. First secretaries bear the burden of work in most embassies. Except in major missions, they tend to be the commercial attachés, information officers, consuls, telegram drafters, executive dogsbodies. In London they head desks looking after individual countries.

Not until he reaches forty can a diplomat reasonably expect promotion to counsellor. This grade, again depending on the size of a mission, normally embraces the head of chancery (an embassy's senior political officer under the ambassador) and the senior commercial post, as well as the head of a geographical or functional department in London. Above counsellor are the glittering heights, the deputy heads of mission ('ministers' in big embassies), the London under-secretaries covering whole continents, and then the ambassadors great and small.

The resulting career structure is the cause of much discussion among British diplomats. The changing nature of diplomatic work has led to an acute shortage of first secretaries and to the holding back in this grade of many first-class diplomats in their late thirties who deserve promotion. At the same time, there is an insufficiency of counsellor posts into which to promote them. Mid-career disillusion has thus become a severe occupational disease of the Diplomatic Service. The 1977 report of the Central Policy Review Staff (the Think-Tank) on the Foreign Office[1] blamed this in part on the high calibre of entrants. It iconoclastically doubted whether this calibre was justified 'by either the importance or the difficulty of the work that the Diplomatic Service does'. Peter Pooley has observed them at each stage in their careers:

Pooley:

I think the British Foreign Office has done extraordinarily well in recruiting at a very high level. They get much more than their fair share of the ablest people as compared with the home civil service or other professions. Their young men under thirty, and in their early thirties, are by and large most impressive. Then something seems to happen, I don't find their top chaps, mark for mark, any more impressive than top chaps in the home civil service or other professions. There is this gap in the middle. Once they have learnt their trade they tend to have a period of being heavily underemployed, not in terms of time but in terms of responsibility. At thirty-five, they still have a long way to go as first secretaries, and as they get up to forty they are still first secretaries and hankering very much for real responsibility. A lot of them may leave at this period through disillusion, a lot may just fail to make the best use of those years, in their personal and professional development, because they are underextended. Therefore, at the age of fifty many will never be as good as they might otherwise have been.

This is a serious criticism and the Foreign Office is aware of it. Like most highly structured professions, it has always insisted on the indivisibility of its 'A' stream intake. It maintains that each diplomat should get his fair share of good and bad post-

---

[1] *Review of Overseas Representation: report by the Central Policy Review Staff*; Chairman: Sir Kenneth Berrill (HMSO, 1977).

ings: the professionalism of the 'Service' depends on it. Yet it has been forced to accept that its best talents will no longer accept being shunted round undemanding jobs, waiting for buggins's turn to become an ambassador. They will simply leave. As a result, it has evolved a complicated, but characteristically meticulous, system for selecting and advancing what it calls 'high fliers' even within the 'A' stream élite. Andrew Wood, head of the personnel department, explains how it works:

Wood:

We have six grades on the current confidential report form, which grade people from outstanding through very effective, through less than adequate, to not up to the job. You get reported on every year. A flier will typically have all outstanding reports, and they will be from a variety of people. This is why you can't identify people as fliers too soon. If someone is posted, to take an example at random, to Islamabad, they might spend four years there always with the same ambassador, who happened to think very well of them, and could get four outstanding reports in a row. Unless that was balanced by a report from Washington, or wherever, which also said that that person was outstanding, you would be very unwise to select them as a flier. So we make a decision about the age of thirty-five, but it is reviewed every year. The initial selection is made within the personnel department, but it is filtered through a system of boards, in which senior members of the Office sit. They are likely to know the people on the list, and to have their own candidates for inclusion too, so there is a fairly thorough discussion. Someone who is close to that grade, but not quite there – what we would call a reserve flier – might have as many very good but not positively outstanding reports as outstanding reports. Once someone has grown their wings, a full flier should be promoted about the age of thirty-eight, in order to fit in the number of posts which will equip him to become ambassador in, let us say, Washington or Bonn before the retirement age of sixty.

A typical Foreign Office flier will usually have done a difficult language and had at least one tough posting to give some respectability to his curriculum vitae. But his stock-in-trade will be a ministerial private office in London, a high-profile conference or negotiation, a good secondment to Cabinet Office or

No. 10, and a mix of the inside track of posts: Paris, Bonn, Brussels and Washington. Fliers will normally have become counsellors well before their fortieth year. Ask them about their envious choice of postings and they will declare they have simply been 'very lucky'.

One diplomat who declares his good luck is Sir Robert Wade-Gery. He began in the chancery in Bonn, returned to private office, then worked on the Cyprus negotiations before going out to run the commercial department in Israel. Since then he has served with the Think-Tank, as minister at the Madrid embassy, as Foreign Office representative in the Cabinet Office, and now High Commissioner in New Delhi. Such a career can seem a fascinating counterpoint between Whitehall and abroad. London is an immersion in the swirl of political events. It is the fighting of constant battles with other Whitehall departments, the exhilaration and the exhaustion of policy formation and revision. Abroad is quite different. It is a time for reflection and for what Sir Robert terms 're-creation':

Wade-Gery:

One of the things that I have noticed about myself and about colleagues and friends in Whitehall is how totally drained intellectually you become after two, three, four years of doing a really high-pressure Whitehall job. I've always found it wonderful at that point, to be able to go off and do something equally active, equally demanding, but demanding in a quite different way. I went off from working in the Think-Tank, feeling absolutely wrung out after three years of trying to live at that pace, to be minister in our embassy in Madrid. It was not a particularly taxing job intellectually, but it was absolutely fascinating because one was learning about an extremely interesting country, about a very interesting people, at an extremely interesting moment of their history. And there was a certain amount of hard tough negotiation as well. Now I actually found that not only very agreeable, but very 're-creative', if that's the right word.

Ambassadorship remains the glittering prize of Diplomatic Service. It is the goal towards which all diplomats openly aspire and is considered a due reward for the hardships which the career can still entail – not least for wives and families. That Sir Robert should regard senior embassy service as 're-creative' might irk those for whom it is the specific object of the diverse career structure which precedes it. Yet the precise qualities required of ambassadorship remain elusive – an issue to which we return in the concluding chapter. Hookey Walker, now ambassador in Abu Dhabi, was formerly head of the personnel operations department and is one of many diplomats fascinated by the question of professional qualifications. He would not disagree with Sir Robert:

Walker:

In all honesty I don't think the job of being an ambassador to one country as opposed to being our man in Brussels, for example, is a job which requires the very highest brain power. I'm not sure how many of our very able under-secretaries want to go off and be an ambassador in a small country. But some do because they are interested in the foreigners about whom they are cerebrating when they are in London. And let's add, there must be a degree, we are all human, of aiming for the glittering lights.

For the bulk of the Diplomatic Service, however, the glittering lights can seem very distant. The prospect is of a series of postings of two to four years' duration, one third of which are normally in London. The dominant complaint is not so much of the substance of this career structure as of its unpredictability. The Service is small and inevitably inflexible, each change of post involving a series of consequential changes, and this chain imposes an intense strain on the diplomatic families it drags behind it. Moves can be sudden, ordered from London at a few weeks' notice, often shortly after a new posting has been taken up. Despite a widespread belief to the contrary, divorce is no more prevalent among diplomats than among other professional groups. Yet it is widely felt that the exigences of the Service – the isolated life, the children's greater need for stability, the subsidised school fees which divorce can jeopardise – disguise many unhappy marriages which at home in Britain would be dissolved. It is startling how many diplomats, particularly in their thirties, seemed surprised at and resentful of this imposed lifestyle, since it is a well-known professional hazard. Mike Jackson, head of chancery in Stockholm, is senior manager of the embassy under the ambassador, and thus responsible for the problems of its staff:

Jackson:

At the age of forty there comes a certain feeling of disillusionment, of rootlessness. A lot of people begin to think, 'Wouldn't it be nice to be in a house for more than three years, to make some real friends, to develop a sense of local community again?' People do transfer out and go to the home civil service on those kind of grounds. There are of course individual difficulties: people get ill, for example, and it's hard to be a diplomat if both the officer and his spouse are not physically fit. We are prone as a Service to marital stress for all kinds of reasons, which can change people's views on how they want to spend their lives. Some of us get problems with drink. That can do the same.

The woes of the diplomatic wife is one of the few controversial topics on which diplomats seem free to express outspoken opinions. Traditionally, the diplomat's wife was expected to follow her husband wherever his career took him. An older generation of wives took it for granted that they would spend their lives in a supportive role to their husbands as they travelled round the world. As ambassadorial wives, they would blossom into a role of their own. It is a full-time job in the public eye, somewhat in the manner of a minor member of the royal family. Yet today's bright young diplomats tend to marry bright young wives with career ambitions of their own. The resulting conflicts are none the easier to bear for being predictable, and certainly the Diplomatic Service exacts a heavy sacrifice from the wives of its officers. David Gore-Booth's wife, Mary, describes her career so far:

Mary Gore-Booth:

In the last six years I think we've been in four different countries. I'm used to packing things up in a couple of weeks, going from sun-dresses to padded-down coats and just adapting. I think that people expect an awful lot from Foreign Office wives. They expect them to behave like an extension of Buckingham Palace. They expect them to be perfect, diplomatic, well-dressed, always available, always smiling, always tactful, remembering everybody's name, never having any problems of their own, always acting as hostess with the door open.

This constant moving around forces the additional strain on husbands and wives of long and often distant separation from their children, most of whom are sent back to boarding school by the age of ten. Mary Gore-Booth found this a particular problem quite distinct from that of a sacrificed career:

Mary Gore-Booth:

At the moment of marrying a Diplomatic Service officer you

do have to decide that you probably won't be able to keep up your doctor's or lawyer's practice, but you never realise what a strain it is to leave your children behind. It's fine while they don't have any problems, and when you're in a country where you can pop back and see them. But it's very difficult not participating in their life, not being there for sports day, not being there if a sudden blank arises and they can't do an exam, or if they suddenly get terribly homesick. What do you do if you're in a country where there's no appropriate school? Leave your husband and stay for the rest of the year with your child, or worry yourself silly and no one gets the benefit? I think that's probably the most difficult part. It's something that a lot of women don't realise because when they marry they don't have children and they think it will be all right.

The Foreign Office offers generous allowances to help with boarding school fees[1] – a policy which is often criticised by Labour Party opponents of private education. But now that it recruits from a wider class background and many diplomats and their wives are not public-school educated, the allowances are regarded by some as a mixed blessing – an 'offer they can't refuse' which makes them dependent on the Service until their children are grown up.

Alan Mooncie is a commercial attaché in Stockholm, who recently decided to bring his children out from England and put them in local schools. His wife Linda explains the reasons why:

Linda Mooncie:

We were just losing touch completely with them – not knowing them in fact. They'd come out for the holidays and it would take a week for them to get used to being back with us and for us to get used to these changed-looking children. Then we would have a week of being together and then the last week would be taken up with preparing for them to go again. Especially in their teenage years, we just felt we didn't know each other any more and it was causing sadness and, I think, a great deal of worry. We felt our influence couldn't be experienced by them as it should be at that time in their development.

---

[1] Fixed at the average of fees at Headmasters' Conference Schools. Bedales is now the most popular secondary school, with Eton in second place.

She is convinced their decision has been frowned on by the Foreign Office and may even limit her husband's career:

Linda Mooncie:

They definitely expect you to send your children off to boarding school and feel it is the best thing for them and therefore the best thing for you maybe; or best for the survival of the Service, or the job. I feel that it's a matter of convenience for them so that the officers can do their job as efficiently as possible. I think that you are being denied a very basic right in being told that it isn't important to be a mother and that it's most important to be a wife.

Stockholm, however, is a comfortable posting compared with some of those which must be filled round the globe. Candidate for the title of worst posting is a topic of heated debate among diplomats: current locations include Lagos, Aden, Hanoi, Beirut and Mogadishu in Somalia, the last being the butt of all diplomatic horror stories. These posts carry extra allowances, more frequent leave, and in most cases, tours of no more than two years' duration. Something of the flavour of the family life in such places is conveyed by Basil Rainbow, a second secretary in Calcutta. He has already done service in Osaka, Darwin, Freetown, Accra and Lahore:

Rainbow:

Living in Calcutta is full of frustration, and for the wife it is also full of boredom. It's not possible for the wife to work here, and there is very little she can do except voluntary work, which in Calcutta isn't of a very congenial nature. So her main problem is filling in her time. During the winter months when it's cool, she can do some of her housework, and she can do a little in the kitchen, but since you employ servants, it isn't straightforward. They are always hovering around. They arrange things differently and they don't like her interfering. In the summer months it is so hot and sticky it is simply impossible to do anything. We have a car, but because of the traffic conditions in Calcutta, and the fact that if there is an accident the driver is quite often attacked, we have a driver who brings me into the office in the morning, then he goes back and he takes my wife shopping. There are no big department stores in Calcutta. There's an open-air market, where you can buy vegetables in season and some basic foodstuffs, but there are a lot of European foodstuffs that you can't get here at all. Some of the shopping, like the buying of the meat, she leaves to the servants, because the conditions in the meat market are so horrible that she can't stand them. They have these large wooden benches and the animals are just cut up there, and all the bits of the animal are left lying about. The vultures are up on the beams, waiting to pounce on anything that's not wanted. You need a strong stomach to go there.

Parallel to the A-stream career structure is the Foreign Office equivalent of the executive, clerical and specialist streams of the home civil service. What is noticeable in the Foreign Office is first, how few of such 'support staff' there are – roughly one per A-streamer – and second, how prominent a part they play in embassy work abroad. Consular officers, communications officers, administrative, secretarial and reception staff are all very much part of the embassy. If the hierarchy is as rigid as that aboard ship, so too is the principle that everyone is engaged in a joint endeavour and that its success will depend on its collective morale. Seasoned Foreign Office inspectors claim to be able to tell if an embassy is 'happy' within five minutes of entering the front door. The cliché of the civil service as a family, absurd in a London department, is not absurd in a small embassy thousands of miles away, in which most staff are by no means the public-school diplomats of popular impression.

The Foreign Office's E-stream corresponds to the home civil service's executive grade. Its officers may well be graduate entrants, and perform administrative, consular, aid, information, personnel and some normal diplomatic work. A-stream diplomats will affirm the E-stream is 'immensely important' and even concede that an E-streamer can do a particular job as well as they can. Yet such is the freemasonry that any fusion of A- and E-streams is firmly resisted. E-streamers are increasingly rising to the rank of first secretary, but the shortage of counsellor posts means they seldom rise further. One E-streamer, David Smallman, has served in Singapore, Nicosia, Islamabad and Aden, and is now first secretary and number two in the embassy in Rangoon. There the ambassador is now the only A-streamer on the staff. David Smallman performs all the functions which an A-stream diplomat would perform in a slightly larger embassy:

Smallman:

I don't regard myself as a different sort of officer, but our career patterns are distinctly different. The structure of the two streams is different, the potential promotion areas are different, and in practice the sort of jobs which most A-stream officers do are different to those jobs which most E-stream officers do. The E-stream officer as he gets more senior is more likely to be involved with administering the Service, whether at home or overseas, whereas the A-stream officer is more likely to be involved in policy formation at home, and direct bilateral political relations abroad.

Smallman sees no reason why some embassies might not in fact be run by E-stream officers. Others, however, are less confident. David Lambert, an E-stream first secretary in Copenhagen, voiced the doubts of many at the continued inflexibility, even class-consciousness, of the Foreign Office career structure:

Lambert:

I certainly couldn't expect to be an ambassador in any post, specially not in any of the larger ones. This is a function of the way in which the service structure operates: it still has two streams and it's difficult for people to break through from the one into the other. I'm not complaining but one has to keep that fundamental difference in mind. So it's unrealistic for anybody in the E-Stream to have as an ambition going somewhere which is out of reach. There is no pyramid in the same way as you have in the home civil service departments, so it follows that you aren't going to have the same sort of rational career structure. All the same, I think the Service has over the years tended to be too wedded to the concept that somebody who comes from Oxford or Cambridge is likely to be automatically better than somebody who doesn't. Consequently, it does seem to me that the Service has masked a good deal of talent.

Some talents masked, other talents wasted: the modern diplomat comes across as a typical bureaucrat, hard-worked if under-stimulated, condemned to a peripatetic career, rigidly graded and exciting only for the lucky few. It is not an appealing image. Yet to the outsider he can seem a well-adjusted, self-assured individual with a distinctive social manner and comfortable lifestyle which he and his wife can take with them wherever they may be sent. These two images are not necessarily incompatible, indeed the one can be a defence mechanism against the other.

A study[1] into the effect of diplomatic life on children, carried out for the Swedish foreign service in 1982, describes the modern diplomat metaphorically as a citizen of a country distinct from his own, which it calls Diplomatia. This country has no physical boundaries, but imposes a fixed code of behaviour on its citizens and sets up strong social and cultural defences against the outside world. The report includes a passage evocative of what some diplomats certainly feel – and what many observers feel about them:

> Living in Diplomatia means being at home everywhere and yet not having a home anywhere. Diplomatia's inhabitants are scattered throughout the world. There is no particular area where most of them live, a place to which they can return and immediately feel at home. There is no 'country' whose geography, climate, urban atmosphere, as well as some of its population, are familiar to them. The inhabitants of Diplomatia seldom settle more than once in the same place. In their minds, they cannot return to their country as if it were an old familiar place, which will always be there within the frontiers of Diplomatia and will always be very much the same. After a time, some people tend to relinquish close contact with their original culture, with the result that Diplomatia becomes their principal place of residence. This is underlined by close friends tending mainly to be residents of Diplomatia. This perspective makes the diplomat 'different' when he or she returns to the country of origin. This disrupts the feeling of belonging and contacts with friends acquired before joining the Foreign Service. The diplomat comes to feel more at home in Diplomatia, and life there becomes increasingly congenial. Diplomatian citizenship is awarded both to the employee and to his or her family. Consequently there are Diplomatian citizens by birth. Sometimes several years can pass before the children see their parents' country of origin for the first time. As a result of the contacts which Diplomatian citizens automatically have across national boundaries, it is not uncommon for them to marry people with different cultural backgrounds from their own.

---

[1] *The Surroundings and Development of Foreign Service Children*, a survey report compiled for the Swedish Ministry for Foreign Affairs by Barbro Hall and Gunnila Masneliez-Steen, 1982.

This dissociation from the mother country and adoption of a
smooth shell as protection from the effects of prolonged residence abroad is acknowledged as the occupational hazard – if
not disease – of diplomacy. It leaves British diplomats vulner-
able to the charge of amateurism, of superficiality and, most
damaging politically, of being better disposed towards foreigners than towards their own countrymen. There has been no
shortage of reports investigating the diplomatic career structure
from the Duncan,[1] Fulton[2] and Think-Tank[3] reports, to
numerous parliamentary committees.[4] Most concentrate on the
need to encourage specialisation and thus give diplomats a
greater sense of intellectual commitment to their work. Families
should suffer less disruption. Diplomats should stay longer in
one place and experience greater interchange with the home
civil service, especially when their children are in secondary
school: a call, in effect, for a drastic reform of the staffing of
first secretary posts. Most such recommendations fall on deaf
ears and many senior diplomats are outspokenly opposed to
them. Sir Julian Bullard has a clear aversion to specialists:

Bullard:

The trouble is they become tremendously well qualified and
experienced and they do almost become indispensable. But
unless somebody wishes to stay in that branch of the Service
throughout his life, and I think most of us would not want
to, there comes a time when the administration would try
to post those people away into a job of a completely different
kind, otherwise they become, so to speak, stuck to the
flypaper forever. I don't think in the long run that is good
for them, and it certainly isn't good for the Service, because
we have to run a mobile, versatile, largely interchangeable
Service in order to staff all these posts that we have.

The Ambassador to Abu Dhabi, Hookey Walker, investigated
each and every reform before concluding that the present
system was unavoidable:

---

[1] *Report of the Review Committee on Overseas Representation* Cmnd 4107; Chairman:
Sir Val Duncan (HMSO, 1969).

[2] *Report of the Committee on the Civil Service* Cmnd 3638; Chairman: Lord Fulton;
5 vols (HMSO, 1968).

[3] *Review of Overseas Representation: report by the Central Policy Review Staff*;
Chairman: Sir Kenneth Berrill (HMSO, 1977).

[4] Committee of Public Accounts, *Economy Measures in the Civil, Military and
Overseas Estates*, Session 1983–4 HCP 106; Chairman: Robert Sheldon (HMSO,
1983) p. xii.

Walker:
I am convinced from having been in the Diplomatic Service for twenty-five years that the right way is to take people into one service and then specialise them through career planning as their innate talents emerge rather than to recruit separately for commercial work, consular work or whatever. One bee in my bonnet is that we should stay longer in our posts. But there are some inbuilt features of our system which make this a darned sight easier to say than to do. At the upper end of our pyramid, one of the difficulties is that we know statistically that a certain number of ambassadors will resign, be retired, be assassinated, or whatever each year, but unfortunately we don't know which ones. You have to move someone to fill the post. By definition you are moving him before you intended to move him, and probably you are setting in train a whole string of moves, all of them earlier than is really desirable.

The permanent secretary, Sir Antony Acland, likewise emphasises diplomacy's need for 'people who are rounded, who have experienced the world as a whole, and not just one part of the world'. While he is sympathetic to the problems of young families and of the counsellor log-jam, neither he nor officials who have served in personnel policy see any way of altering the structure. Any change risks, as they would put it, throwing out the baby of a unified élite profession with the bathwater of personal inconvenience. Even a young recruit professes the system's virtues. Gordon Reid in Budapest acknowledges the demands which Diplomatia makes on its citizens and is prepared to take it on those terms:

Reid:
My hesitation in joining the Foreign Office for about two or three years was partly because I felt perhaps I was not the right type. Having joined the Office, my fears have been in a sense allayed. There's no doubt that a diplomat has a certain style, a certain smoothness, I think that's fair comment. My own intention, my declared intention having joined the Service, is not to change. I shall remain me. However, one has to knock off the edges in places, there are certain times when you have to act in a certain way, and be able to do it, and perhaps if I may use the word 'act' and dwell on it, that is what it's about in part. I'm willing to, and want to, acquire the tools of the job.

This professional conservatism is rampant throughout most of the Foreign Service – often, as Sir Oliver Wright said, for good operational reasons. We consider the price paid for it in the concluding chapter. Now we turn to the job for which Gordon Reid is acquiring the tools, the work of the embassy abroad.

A Patch of Britain

Wherever you may be, Her Britannic Majesty's embassy is a little patch of England. The royal coat of arms is on the gate. Some small architectural feature, a discreet portico or an ornamental lawn, will indicate a more than ordinary building. Yet the style is not grand: foyer and waiting room are Ministry of Works, late-1950s' vintage. There are nylon-covered chairs, a rack of export magazines, some back copies of *The Times*, a neat colour photograph of the Queen or Prince Charles en famille. The scene is presided over by a security guard with an earthy provincial accent and a dozen stories of his time in the Royal Navy.

Penetrate a little further and you will encounter the embassy's human face. The consul is a jovial, if long-suffering character. His knowledge of the pitfalls facing Britons abroad is exhaustive. The commercial attaché is eager but inexperienced: recently arrived from a one-week marketing course in the north of England. His stock-in-trade are brochures and telephone numbers. The chancery staff are more assured, priding themselves on their knowledge of the political scene, smooth to a fault. The military attaché will fill those awkward social silences with a quip and a ready drink. The ambassador himself is carefully friendly, as the British are with those to whom they are not properly introduced. An embassy is the personification of its ambassador. He sets its tone as a captain does that of a ship.

Yet to many people, embassies can seem an unnecessary extravagance. In an age of jet travel, electronic communication and simultaneous translation, it is less easy to justify a worldwide network of local offices, most still offering a diplomatic table d'hôte. If ministers or officials in London need to deal with opposite numbers in Bonn or Tokyo, they can surely telephone or fly out in person. The tourist industry can be supplied with consular services on a contract basis, as could commercial firms in need of local advice and contracts. For cultural and educational ties, there is the British Council and a plethora of societies for promoting relations between Britain and every country in the world. Who needs embassies?

In the first place, embassies differ. Britain now has 213 posts abroad, including missions to multilateral organisations. This total has increased drastically since decolonisation. Some, such as Washington and the European Economic Community, are unlike any others and will be dealt with in the next chapter. But the vast majority bear at least a passing resemblance to our opening caricature. Those who work in them are naturally enthusiastic about their purpose. Peter Unwin is ambassador in Budapest:

Unwin:

Just take this country, for example. It only has ten million people, but they are ten million very lively, intelligent, innovative people, people to whom we sell seventy or eighty million pounds' worth of goods each year, people of whom it is worth having a proper understanding, a good cultural understanding, a good information understanding. And even if we had no contribution to make to the formulation of foreign policy – and I can see relatively little – I think there is a real job to be done of promoting Britain's interests in Hungary.

Nick Fenn may be ambassador on the other side of the globe, in Rangoon, but his definition of his post is in fact almost identical:

Fenn:

We need an embassy in Burma because of its enormous economic potential, because of its strategic political position, and because of its uncertain future, and for these three reasons it seems to me that we should have someone here. There are in fact only eight UK-based staff [that is sent from London as against locally engaged] to cover the three main jobs. You need somebody to organise the export promotion; you need somebody to keep a watch on what's going on politically; and you need somebody to look after British people who visit. In addition to that you clearly need somebody to run the place, and administration in Rangoon is very often a complex and cumbersome business. The rest are here to support that, communicators and secretaries and so on. But you have to consider the question of historical incubus. This has been a major embassy of a former imperial power, and there are great expectations of what this embassy should do. We can no longer remotely measure up to those expectations, but of course we do our best.

Sir John Nicholas, High Commissioner in Colombo, finds more specific benefits from the links established abroad:

Nicholas:

Selling Britain sounds as if I'm selling Stratford-on-Avon or modern technology. I'm not doing that. The people here in Sri Lanka, the people at the top, are terribly well aware of Britain. The television programmes and the newspapers are full of items from Britain. They go to Britain a lot. Like any high commissioner or ambassador one is pursuing British interests in a broad sense. It is, for instance, in our interest that Sri Lanka develops economically, remains democratic and remains, maybe non-aligned, but Western-oriented rather than Soviet-oriented or Chinese-oriented. We managed to get them with us on the General Assembly vote in the Falklands debate, and I put that down to the good relations we have with them, not to any logical consideration of their own interests.

The job of a modern bilateral embassy is to keep London informed of developments in a particular foreign country, to liaise with its government and to represent Britain's commercial and other interests there. It is thus part public relations office, part news agency, part messenger service. In some places, one function will predominate over others. For the Foreign Secretary, Sir Geoffrey Howe, embassies are an essential tool of his trade, two-way communications posts for the transmission of British foreign policy:

Howe:

I think that the British Foreign Office probably tends to use its embassies more often and more effectively than some of its counterparts. For finding out about things we use them a lot. I often find myself saying, 'Well, we'd better send in so and so to find out about that,' talking about one's ambassador in a capital. Or on a longer-term basis, 'Look, this is an exercise which we've really got to get across to our partners in the Community. So we shall have to make sure that our ambassadors are carefully briefed and present the thing in a methodical fashion.' I think we use our embassies a great deal more than other people use their embassies in London, particularly for transmitting messages to foreign governments.

Reporting to the Foreign Office in London constitutes the bulk of the political work of most embassies. Peter Unwin in

Budapest describes how his embassy goes about the task of fulfilling this requirement:

Unwin:

What an embassy knows ought to be the iceberg and the one eighth of the iceberg that shows above the surface ought to be what we report back. One goes about assembling a lot of knowledge, a lot of information, and a lot of insights about a subject, and every so often one draws those together into a report. That applies to what you might call the long-term subjects like 'How is Hungarian reform getting on?' Of course more fast-moving subjects like Hungarian attitudes towards deployment of the Soviet weapons in Eastern Europe are watched on a day-by-day basis. Any developments are reported fast. But I have to add that, whereas in the West you are tending to read newspapers, here you're tending to read the tea leaves.

The product of this activity is the telegram, either wired or carried back and forth to London by Queen's messengers in the regular 'diplomatic bag'. Hundreds pour into the Foreign Office daily, to be noted, digested, sometimes drawn to ministers' attention, but more often shelved without being read by anyone above a desk officer. Yet the attention given to telegrams at source is intense:

Unwin:

When we've assembled information, we usually write it down. There's an old jibe that the civil service writes too much down, but I don't agree with that myself. We gradually assemble a collective knowledge of the subject, and then we tend to have a meeting to decide how we'll go about turning that mass of information into something which is worth sending to London. The people in London don't need everything we need, they need the essentials. We send something to London very nearly every day, but we send a fairly major piece about once a fortnight.

Sir John Nicholas in Colombo illustrates how important even the most mundane political reporting can be when suddenly an embassy finds that its country is appearing on every front page back home:

Nicholas:

Our task is to ensure that our desk in the Foreign Office's South Asia department fully understands all the background to what is happening here politically and economically, so that when something happens like the violence in July[1] and we suddenly become headline news, we don't suddenly have to start explaining everything from the beginning. They know virtually what we know, maybe not in such detail, but they understand the whole background, so it's then very easy to communicate with them when there are problems. But that isn't the only reason why political reporting is necessary. The Foreign Office is the custodian of information about countries throughout the world, and we have to keep them aware of what is going on. They have to brief ministers, maybe very quickly, sometimes without the time to consult us. They have to answer questions in the House. They must be prepared when the next crisis in the world arises.

The volume of embassy reporting is controversial. It is frustrating for able diplomats to spend much of their time composing reports which are doctored by embassy superiors, sent off to London and, for all they hear of them, ignored. It is the more frustrating when they know ministers read the newspapers over breakfast and may well place greater reliance on an instant (and perhaps inaccurate) press account of an event in their country than on their careful analysis. French embassies are known even to await the publication of *Le Monde* before writing their telegrams, so as to know what their minister has already read. British embassies are regarded by the diplomatic community as masters of the reporting art. But a lengthy analysis of Swedish trade unions or a two-page report on the visit of Chou En-lai's widow to Rangoon does not necessarily contribute to even the longer-term formulation of foreign policy in London. One ex-ambassador to both Paris and Washington, Sir Nicholas Henderson, has strong views on the subject:

Henderson:

This is one of the curious things if you serve abroad: you're like the scrum-half in a rugger team. You get the ball out of the scrum with some difficulty, often with a lot of people heeling rather badly, you whip it to London, but you've no idea what happens down the three-quarter line, whether it's kicked into touch, passed on to someone else, or scores a

---

[1] Riots between the Tamils and Sinhalese erupted in Sri Lanka on 23 July 1983 and lasted until the end of August, resulting in approximately 400 deaths. Violence flared again in July 1984.

try. All that does happen, sometimes, not regularly, is that a long time after you sent what you regard as a moving despatch, you get a very short letter from the head of the department who's responsible for the country you're in, saying your despatch has been read with much interest by those concerned. You never know whether it's been read by the Foreign Secretary or what anybody thinks of it.

Constant efforts are made by London to reduce the amount of reporting from embassies. What is so difficult, as Sir John Nicholas found, is to know what might be useful – albeit sitting on a London shelf – should a crisis suddenly break. Britain's embassy in Buenos Aires in early 1982 was a diplomatic backwater. Yet every sentence of its telegrams and messages to London was picked over by the Franks inquiry when it came to investigate the background to the Falklands invasion. The same happened to the Barbadian high commission after Grenada. One embassy in no doubt about the market for its reporting has been Beirut. The ambassador, David Miers, knows his output is devoured by the Foreign Office machine – the more so when Britain had troops on the ground in Lebanon in early 1984:

Miers:

Obviously the situation in Beirut is such that it is frequently in the news in Britain and ministers are therefore concerned about what's happening here. So you find that your views are sought, and you are expected to comment at greater length and more detail than you would if you were in another part of the world where attention isn't focused so keenly as it is here. What you say and write is given more respect and more automatic distribution. As ambassador, when you visit home you obviously have access to the Secretary of State or even to the Prime Minister, which you wouldn't have as head of a Foreign Office department.

Ambassadors such as David Miers, caught up in a serious international crisis, invariably look back on such moments as the high point of their careers. After years of anonymity, an ambassador is the one civil servant entitled to regard himself as the centre of political attention. He becomes more than just a conduit of advice and information. He is the representative of Britain. Humiliated in Peking, kidnapped in Buenos Aires, surrounded constantly with armed guards in Beirut, the ambassador is the embodiment of the nation, and his demeanour under pressure must reflect it. During the recent Libyan embassy siege, the ambassador in Tripoli and his wife, Oliver and Julia Miles, became public figures, interviewed daily on the radio.

Out of the public eye, however, the political work of an embassy can seem a less rewarding task. Unless there is a ministerial visit in the offing or a forthcoming negotiation to prepare for, it is a matter of a routine of foreign ministry contacts and communications with a desk officer in London. Adrian Fortescue was posted from the frenetic political life of Washington to the embassy in Budapest. Here he found the embassy's role in the great issues of East-West relations less than prominent:

Fortescue:

I suppose the biggest single difference is that in Washington you are dealing with a government whose actions have a direct bearing on world events, and are of concern to everybody, particularly to a close ally like the UK. There is no comparable dialogue with the Hungarians. Our relationship is one that we can foster and try to foster, but if we say something to our Hungarian interlocutors about what their governments might be doing, we can't fool ourselves into thinking that it is going to change the world if they don't do it. What's more, the whole dialogue takes place in the shadow of the superpower relationship. What we say to the Hungarians may or may not convince them; they may or may not pass it on to the Russians; but there is no reason to think that even if they do, it is going to change Russian policy.

In such places, the embassy's chancery, its political department, is essentially the Foreign Office's insurance policy. It is cover against the risk of being caught short in a crisis. Cabinet or parliament must never be left demanding, 'What was the Foreign Office doing?' when revolution occurs or British citizens are arrested or a tourist goes missing. Hence the elaborate edifice of high-calibre diplomats doing often tedious work, of postings switched frequently to maintain freshness, of expensive language training and the constant round of hospitality. You never know what might happen.

Yet political work is only part of a diplomat's job, and to some a decreasingly important part. The function most regularly demanded of an embassy is more mercantile: selling Britain, and particularly Britain's exports. Until reorganisation in the 1940s, this was the responsibility of a separate commercial consular service. By the 1960s this had changed radically. Commercial work became crucial, as much to the diplomat's reputation as to the vitality of the British economy. The actual work performed by a commercial attaché naturally varies. In Western Europe he may do little more than peddle a list of commercial contacts and help the Department of Trade stage its exhibitions. In communist countries – indeed in most states with a broadly corporatist industrial structure – he will be closely involved in any bilateral contract with state purchasing organisations.

In the Gulf, commercial work is central to the activity of every mission. This area of long-standing British influence should be fertile ground for British industrialists and financiers. Yet businessmen must adhere to unfamiliar, baffling and frequently corrupt codes of commercial behaviour to have any hope of success. It is the ideal environment for an experienced and effective commercial attaché. One such is Roger Huxley, whose bailiwick covers the United Arab Emirates. His job, as he describes it, is that of superior nanny to the British businessman abroad:

Huxley:

Many British businessmen who come to this particular market are not aware of the dos and don'ts of doing business in Abu Dhabi. We have a role in educating them. We also have a major role in finding out what business opportunities there are for British companies. This is a particularly difficult market, in that many major buyers of goods and services don't issue their requirements by public tender, so one has to find out about them. One has to go round on calls, meeting engineers, meeting managers of oil companies, of the power service, of the sewerage authorities. Sewerage is worth about £55 million per year in Abu Dhabi alone. One hears when jobs are about to come up, and one broadcasts the fact to as many British companies as one can. This is primarily done through the export intelligence service which is operated by the Department of Trade in London, a computerised service which relays business opportunities to as many British companies as are subscribers to it. British businessmen very often have not researched the market adequately before they come. They don't know the basic requirements of the market. They very often have never been to an Arab country before. One of the major functions of a commercial officer is to direct them to the best local contacts to try and arrange an agent or representative or possibly a joint venture partner, and we can advise on this. So we act as a sort of marriage agency.

What that means in practice is doing what any salesman does, going out to call on potential customers. Huxley describes a typical working day:

Huxley:

Last Wednesday I had five calls organised on businessmen round Abu Dhabi. Two of them were absolutely first-rate. One was on an oil company, which told me its next two-year programme of expenditure and came up with seven major projects which we didn't know about, approaching almost $2 million. That was a commercial officer's dream. I also saw a chap who wants to represent British companies. He's selling oilfield equipment: very good local company, not large, hard-working, with some good agencies already. I'm going to recommend it to any companies who want to come in and sell this sort of thing. I called on an agricultural supplier whom I know well, one of my contacts. When people ask me agricultural questions I usually go to him, so we had a chat and a cup of coffee. I had a call on another oil company, I hung around for half an hour, drinking coffee; the chap didn't turn up. I went away to another call, on an agent. The man had been called away on business, but I sat drinking coffee again with his secretary who told me a couple of little goodies, but nothing special.

Many commercial opportunities depend heavily on financial packages in which aid and government guarantees play an important part. Piecing together such packages inevitably involves local embassy personnel whose relations with local civil servants can be crucial to the success of a contract. The embassy becomes commercial agent to the whole British government machine. Sir John Nicholas in Colombo was thus drawn in to a British consortium bid for a local airport project:

Nicholas:

The present runway at the airport is breaking up so they have to have a new runway, and they have gone out to international tender. There are sixteen tenders in. The lowest

British bid is about £127 million and the lowest bid of all is the Japanese bid. But now we get down to the problem of getting together a financial package, because at the end of the day, even if a rival's price isn't as low, their financial package can be more attractive. If we could persuade the Overseas Development Agency and the Department of Trade to provide some Aid and Trade Provision – that is a segment of the aid programme which is used directly to assist British firms to win overseas contracts in competition with other foreign firms – it could help enormously. They have got to be competitive, but you won't win a tender here, with a country in the economic and financial position this one is in, unless you have a good financial package. That's the secret.

Derek Davies is chairman of the consortium, the UK Airports Group, and a director of GEC Electrical Projects Ltd, who are leaders in the current Colombo Airport Project. He acknowledges the help that the high commission has given his team:

Davies:

We met what is known as unfair competition when quoting for the job, inasmuch as the Japanese offered extended terms, something like thirty years' credit, with 3¼% interest, with a ten-year moratorium. But we could only obtain a usual-buyer credit from the Export Credit Guarantee Department, which has a consensus rate of about nine per cent at the moment. We think that this is unfair competition. The government do have an extra allocation of money, known as ATP, which is Aid and Trade Provision Fund, which they can draw on in these circumstances. In this particular case, Her Majesty's Government agreed to let us have 25.1% of the UK goods and services value of this particular contract to help us compete with the Japanese. The high commission were very helpful indeed. Both the commercial counsellor and the high commissioner took a great interest and managed to obtain on our behalf proof of what the Japanese were doing, which is essential if we are going to get Aid and Trade Provision.[1]

Nonetheless, the commercial work of British embassies abroad comes in for frequent criticism. They are charged with

---

[1] The story had a happy ending. The British consortium won the Colombo Airport Project from the Japanese.

amateurism and inexperience and there have been suggestions they would be better run direct from the Trade Department or some other organisation than from the Foreign Office. Derek Davies finds the quality of the service varies from country to country:

Davies:

It's the experience that makes the difference. It's most unfair to expect diplomats to be able to promote business for the UK unless they have had some form of training. We, as experts in obtaining business overseas, spend a long time studying the principles of marketing, whereas a diplomat does not have the time in his normal job to undertake such training. Businessmen feel that more training should be given to diplomats to enable them to help us more. I think some of them would rather not go out looking for business, but just greet businessmen when they arrive in the country, and talk nicely to them. In fact we want the dynamic types, who are interested in obtaining business for the UK and will do more than just read newspapers and send home cuttings of invitations to tender. Really it does boil down to the diplomatic staff taking a much bigger interest in helping business. The days of gunship diplomacy are over and our embassies, like those of our competitor countries, especially Japan and some continental countries, must go out and become salesmen.

This applies as much in Europe as in the third world. Denis Dunstone is head of BP's operation in Copenhagen. If the Foreign Office really wants to engage in export promotion, he argues, it cannot do it just as an information bureau:

Dunstone:

The problem with the commercial section is that they are too passive and responsive to outside events in the execution of their role. Maybe that is what is expected of them, but I believe that it would be a more dynamic and effective organisation if it were more goal-oriented, if there were plans and objectives which were agreed and had to be met, and if the people employed in the commercial section could work towards definite targets.

Unflattering comparisons are made by many observers with the highly interventionist French diplomats, or with the German commercial service, mostly staffed by non-diplomats and run by the German chamber of commerce. What irks such businessmen is that many diplomats fail to appreciate their own limitations, thinking themselves polished salesmen. Commercial work has become so important a qualification that every rising star is expected to have had commercial 'experience', irrespective of aptitude or training, at some point in his career. Kim Sullivan is a Mandarin Chinese expert trying to help businessmen sell goods in Stockholm (he also speaks Swedish). He has no doubt of the purpose of this phase of his career:

Sullivan:

I'm an amateur in a job which I think has been specially designed for, or has developed into a job for, amateurs over the years. I am surrounded by professionals here, who are the locally engaged staff in the embassy – and I'm working with professionals in London and at the British end, those employed by UK industries and the people in the Department of Trade and Industry. Of course one is also dealing with professionals here in Sweden, both in the government institutions and in industry. But if one day I become an ambassador, having done this job will make me a much more professional ambassador than I would have been had I had a more limited experience.

Some commercial officers are dismayed by the implication that the job is essentially a training for ambassadorship: that any competent diplomat should be able to do a commercial job on two or three weeks' training and before moving on to higher things. Meanwhile, any diplomat who shows a particular flair for the work cannot stay with it lest he risk losing promotion. Roger Huxley in Abu Dhabi has built a solid reputation in the labyrinths of Gulf commerce and has managed to hold on to a job he clearly loves for four years. But he knows he must leave soon if he is to advance in his profession of diplomat – whatever loss it may imply to his embassy's effectiveness as an aid to businessmen:

Huxley:

I would like to see more professionalism in the training of commercial officers. I was certainly not happy with the way I was prepared for my job. This is perhaps Foreign Office heresy, but personally I would like to see a career structure for commercial people. Only commercially orientated officers, I think, can talk to businessmen at their level.

The establishment disagrees. Many senior diplomats feel the Service went too far in its emphasis on commercial work in the

1960s and 1970s. To them, the job of an embassy is essentially the promotion of good relations, the building of mutual confidence on which political liaison and sound policy can be based. This is not, and should not be, compatible with the wholly different skill of salesmanship. Even the head of a basically commercial mission, Hookey Walker, in Abu Dhabi, does not disagree. In what is now a standard Foreign Office maxim, he points out that:

Walker:

Contracts are not won by embassies or even ministers making political pitches. You win your contracts by offering the right product at the right time and at the right price.

Whatever the importance of the commercial work of a modern embassy, he says, it must ultimately be subordinate to the political:

Walker:

We would put the commercial aim first, although personally I am dubious about the dividing lines between commercial work and political work, or even between commercial work and defence work. But I think that there have been some events in recent history that show it's dangerous to go overboard on what the Diplomatic Service calls commercial work. For example, it doesn't do you much good to urge your businessmen to invest in a country or urge them to win big contracts in a country, if you then have a revolution, as happened in Iran. So I think that political work is fundamental, but as a necessary base for commercial work.

Such diplomats see the commercial function of an embassy as strictly intermediary. It is to supply political and economic briefing, make introductions and lay the groundwork for salesmanship. Selling should be left to outside experts whose companies stand to profit by it. The Foreign Office, ever defensive on this subject, points out that it now charges fees for its overseas commercial service.[1] Most of its customers tend to be small or first-time businessmen who have yet to find their feet locally. It can reasonably claim its customers are satisfied, if they continue to use the service.

---

[1] They charge £150 for the Market Prospects Service, £23 for the Overseas Status Report Service, and £100 for the Export Representative Service. The fees are mainly intended to deter casual inquiries: where, for example, any of the recommended businessmen are visited by the applicant within six months of receiving the report, they are refunded.

The other work of an embassy comes in for fewer brickbats. Information officers – their numbers drastically reduced under recent cuts – are quite simply press and public relations officers to the embassy. They monitor local newspapers and prepare digests for the staff. They will often use local translators. Their chief complaint is that the work, which involves keeping in touch with local journalists and information ministries and disseminating 'good news about Britain', can be routine and uninspiring. As in so much of embassy work, it is remarkable how high a calibre of official is often assigned to this task. The Foreign Office must have more information officers with first-class degrees than the whole of British industry.

Half-sister to the embassy is the consular service, coping with the tribulations of British citizens abroad, and alternately assisting or holding back (according to government policy) the flood of foreigners wanting to come to Britain. It is the aspect of embassy work which the public most often sees. Many would regard it as the chief justification for British representation abroad, especially in countries such as Spain and France with large numbers of tourists, and in Commonwealth countries with continuing close links with Britain.

Consular officers, many of them drawn from the E-stream of the Service, must be jacks-of-all-trades. They may be visiting a drug offender in a Turkish gaol; helping repatriate a bankrupt tourist from the Costa Brava; seeking to determine the right to a passport of a 'patrial' from the Punjab; advancing some money to a stranded sailor in New York. Times are not always what they were. The British Consul in Calcutta has a map of East Bengal on his wall with pins marking the location of every British citizen. He reflects sadly that they once marked whole British communities. Yet in Europe business is booming. In France the consular service recently arranged emergency supplies to stranded British lorry drivers in the Alps. Last year, Spain yielded over 500 'serious' consular cases from tourists in trouble. For these services charges are usually levied. James Mellon's chief problem, as ambassador in Copenhagen, is little more than an occasional football hooligan. But he knows what happens if his service is not up to scratch:

Mellon:

It's very difficult to be dogmatic about consular work, it varies all over the world. In some places I have seen young British consular officers go into very dangerous situations

59

and come out with the British businessmen that they had been sent in to get. I wouldn't like to exaggerate and say that we have any of these problems in Denmark. But if the suggestion is that we should therefore give up consular work here, you would have to look at the kind of pressures that are on us. For example, people may not be very sympathetic to football fans that go amok in the UK, but if it happens abroad, in Europe, there is some old mum who is going to be rightly worried about her little boy who has been locked up. Until you can persuade the public and, frankly, parliament, not to be interested in that sort of case, don't ask me not to be interested in it.

Much embassy work is not performed by career diplomats at all but by other officials on secondment. This may include the administration of aid projects, defence relations, the admission of Commonwealth immigrants, labour matters and cultural relations. The defence staff – in larger missions divided into military, naval and air attachés – must often marry the job of arms sales with that of intelligence and liaison. It is not an easy marriage, especially in small embassies where there are only one or two on the job. Observers such as the Think-Tank have advocated a drastic curtailment of the Service attaché system, with a concentration on countries where there is a manifest intelligence, liaison or defence sales role to perform. The Foreign Office, always glad of an extra pair of hands, keeps out of this argument, since the attachés are financed by the Ministry of Defence. Diplomacy – even if it means no more than arranging courtesy visits for British ships – provides a useful job for senior officers where no other promotion is available. But there are many within the Ministry of Defence who view the attaché service with scepticism. It is a case of Britain playing a diplomatic game, in part because the rest of the world is doing so.

A large amount of embassy work still takes the form of human intercourse: both conversation between diplomats and in the context of diplomatic entertainment. Great efforts are therefore made to stimulate and facilitate it. Hospitality is conducted at public expense, with the exception of the imputed labour of diplomatic wives. Depending on the country, a diplomat may spend three or four evenings a week at official functions, cocktails or dinner parties. He must maintain a house – for which he receives an allowance which also covers ministry-approved dinner service, glass and silver – appropriate for his status and its scale of hospitality. He is representing not only the embassy but the British government and people. Ambassadors officially represent the monarch and even take precedence over the prime minister on embassy territory. Sir Nicholas Henderson sums up this aspect of his job:

Henderson:

One of the odd things about the Foreign Office is that you're asked or expected to be able to play completely different parts: sometimes humorous, sometimes tragic, sometimes great, sometimes small. The British ambassador in most countries will be a very important person – he will stand out in the crowd and will be looked to. Therefore you can't hide anybody in the job. You can't say, 'He's not much good, this fellow, he's given some pretty bad advice, he doesn't seem to be very active or dynamic in Whitehall, let's send him to some distant place.' A distant place, oddly enough, may be an area where the British ambassador cuts considerable ice, for historical reasons, or just because Britain is a country with world influence and a world language.

Of all the aspects of an embassy's work, the representational is the least quantifiable – and therefore the most open to misunderstanding and ridicule. Many of its activities, perhaps even most, are a waste of time, energy and money. But how to tell which? At what point on the cost curve should a halt be called? For instance, no subject so obsesses the Foreign Office's critics as much as its buildings.[1] British embassies and residences are still probably the grandest, or at least the most distinguished architecturally, in the world. The reasons are entirely historical. Most have long since been paid for and, assuming Britain means to maintain a representational presence in most world capitals, are effective instruments of national projection. In cities not blessed with a free embassy property market (which means most), they could be replaced only at enormous cost. In addition, most embassy staff live in conditions far worse than they would be enjoying in London, with the added disadvantage of renting rather than owning their temporary homes. A friendly ambassador's residence (and its swimming pool) is

---

[1] For a typical example, see: Committee of Public Accounts, *Economy Measures in the Civil, Military and Overseas Estates*, 1983–4 HCP 106 (HMSO, 1983) p. xii.

often a refuge for everyone. Property extravagance is the least of the charges reasonably levelled at the diplomatic door. Nick Fenn is ambassador in Rangoon. His embassy dominates the city's waterfront next to the famous Strand Hotel. His residence is a delightful and no less spacious villa set in cool lawns near the centre of town:

Fenn:

We bought this very nice house and the chancery building in 1949. Foreigners may no longer acquire property in Rangoon, and if we were to sell it the Burmese government has the right of pre-emptive purchase at the price we paid for it in 1949, which is plainly an uneconomic proposition. I reckon we would spend what we would get for this splendid house in two or three years' rent on a modest villa in the suburbs where many of our diplomatic colleagues have to live. That is plainly absurd. If one is going to try to maintain Britain's standing in circumstances of this kind, there is room for a little panache. That's why I greatly value the Daimler, which is widely admired in Rangoon, and why I think the splendid diplomatic instrument which is this house ought to be retained.

In Stockholm, the ambassador, Sir Donald Murray, is equally proud of a mansion as handsome as any in that city of fine houses. It is opposite the English church, with its garden stretching down to the water, on which the ambassador may sail in summer and ski in winter:

Murray:

The people who come to this house, mostly of course Swedish but British as well, expect and hope to see something of Britain inside. I think they do, whether it is the portraits of kings and queens on the walls, or whether it is the furniture or the style. They judge Britain to a certain extent by this.

Embassy entertainment is a different matter. A much-observed feature of diplomatic hospitality is that it frequently appears to involve diplomats entertaining each other. This is defended in countries with closed regimes where contact with local people is hard: diplomatic receptions which locals are 'permitted' to attend can be a rare opportunity to pick up information, even gossip, about the government and its intentions. However, in most countries inviting fellow diplomats round for drinks or dinner at the taxpayers' expense can seem a weak form of intelligence gathering and a condemnation of the diplomats' oft-proclaimed expertise at 'getting on with foreigners'. Nor is the Foreign Office's preferred form of hospitality, the cocktail or dinner party, a particularly convincing one. Encounters at such gatherings are brief and superficial and the presence of wives, many not speaking the same language, inevitably inhibits 'shop' talk. This is especially so given the convention that men should not sit next to each other at the dinner table. Sir John Nicholas, in Colombo, acknowledges some short-comings of diplomatic protocol:

Nicholas:

Quite frankly, it is only by meeting people socially that you get the sort of relationship that you are seeking. You'll never establish it by just going to visit people in their offices. I entertain quite a lot, although I never have to say to myself, 'It's time I had a dinner party.' It's always for a specific reason. I had a visiting MP recently, so I had a largish dinner party for him. When the Birmingham Chamber of Commerce came, I had a stag reception with just businessmen, people they wanted to meet. I wouldn't like to say that the wives get in the way, that would be unfair, but sometimes I do rather feel that. I have often thought that the way we sit people at table means that I spend the entire dinner talking to the two leading wives and my wife has the two leading men. Sometimes I wish it was the other way round.

David Gore-Booth also finds much diplomatic entertaining an unsatisfactory way of doing business, even in the comparatively relaxed social atmosphere of the UN in New York:

Gore-Booth:

There is a great deal of diplomatic life which is irksome, just as there are many countries in the world which are irksome. I do find the social side of the thing tedious and so does my wife: not, I hasten to say, the concept of entertaining in itself which I think is a valuable – indeed essential – part of the business. But I myself prefer contact with people over lunch or over dinner rather than propped up in some great ball-room where there are a lot of other people and you get stuck in purely empty chit-chat. In these circumstances you can't really have an off-the-record conversation, and actually off-the-record conversations are the stuff of diplomacy.

Many younger diplomats say they would prefer a straightfor-ward expense account as available to home civil servants (up to a limited point), with freedom to judge a 'well-aimed lunch' against yet another stage-army at a cocktail party. As it is, they feel their colleagues are always watching to see that they – and their wives – are pulling their social weight within the embassy circuit. And it remains inevitable that the higher a diplomat moves up the embassy ladder, the more representational his work and the less he can structure it to his own tastes. An ambassador's life can be a punishing round of official occasions of minimal political value. Yet appearances must be maintained if offence is not to be caused. Sir Robert Wade-Gery in Delhi:

Wade-Gery:
Certainly major visitors take up a great deal of my time, and I am very glad they do; it seems to me a very important and central part of what one is doing. The social side of life goes on fairly continuously in the sense that one goes to a lot of parties, which are a useful tool of the trade. It's a way of getting to know people in what, when I arrived, was a new country to me, and of keeping in touch with people when you do know them. A lot of entertaining we do in this house is purposive in the sense that it is focused on the visit of a minister, or of the Chairman of ICI or whoever it may be. I sometimes wish that we had more time and resources in this house to do more what you might call initiative entertaining rather than responsive entertaining.

For the ambassador's wife, life can be no less busy – and no less representational. Lady Wade-Gery describes a typical day at the Indian high commission:

Lady Wade-Gery:
On Monday morning we already had Mr and Mrs Norman Tebbit[1] staying with us, so the day began with a briefing meeting here for the minister with members of the high commission. Quite often when we have briefing meetings here in the house we invite the wives of our own members of staff to come and meet the wife of the visitor who is being briefed. It is very valuable for everybody and great fun for the girls to be included. In the evening we had the Director of the Washington National Gallery and his wife, who were out here to do some investigation because the Festival of India is going to America next year. He had come to look at things to borrow, and was a great friend of friends. Then

---

[1] Norman Tebbit, Secretary of State for Trade and Industry from 1983.

we went out to an official dinner being given for Mr Tebbit in the evening. So on that day there was the morning meeting, people to lunch, people to drinks, dinner out. Tuesday morning at 11 o'clock, I went to call on the wife of a colleague to talk about the Delhi Flower Show, which is run by the YWCA to make money for their village projects. The Delhi Flower Show is quite old and traditionally diplomats, particularly British diplomats, have been involved in running it.

Her support staff would be the envy of her contemporaries in the home civil service (and in most of the Foreign Office too):

Lady Wade-Gery:

It breaks down into a cook and a boy, three sweepers, who are the people who do all the cleaning, and five bearers who are a mixture of housemaids and a butler. They wait at table and look after the house. We have a driver of our own. We have a laundryman, and his wife who irons. How many is that? And five gardeners. Now that sounds a great many, and that is the one area perhaps where in England you would manage even on a garden this size with far fewer. But this is how the country works. The garden is wholly non-mechanised, we have no mechanical equipment of any kind at all, and in India you aim to employ a lot of people. It's a very poor country, wages by European standards are very low, and so it is not as extravagant as it sounds.

British embassies and the gracious lifestyle which continues within their walls may indeed be superb 'tools of the trade' of representational diplomacy. Yet ask an Indian or Hungarian or Arab or American what conditions his attitude to Britain and the British people, and the reply is unlikely to relate to anything emanating from a British embassy. It might once have done – when communications were limited and diplomacy was a matter of élites talking to élites. Today, international relations properly so called are based on diverse influences: the media, tourism, sport, educational exchanges, migrant labour and the increasing cosmopolitanism of culture. Much of this is inevitably beyond the reach of embassies or diplomacy, but not all of it need be so. The new 'alternative diplomacy' is that of the international media and public relations, of student exchanges, of world broadcasting, or professional secondments. The media are particularly important in conditioning political attitudes abroad, the more so as press freedom diminishes and journalists are increasingly considered by totalitarian governments as proxy diplomats. The London correspondent of a foreign newspaper probably has more impact on his government's view of Britain than does that government's ambassador in London. A British embassy must struggle forlornly to correct any misconceptions he may have peddled.

The implications of this 'alternative diplomacy' can consume an embassy's time and energy. No amount of fostering good relations can compensate for a mob of football fans on the rampage in Brussels, or the widely-publicised body-search of an Indian girl at Heathrow, or a casual reference to a Pakistani hotel by an English cricketer. Months of patient diplomacy were undone by the film, *Death of a Princess*,[1] about Saudi Arabia. A Granada Television biography of the Bengali nationalist Subhas Chandra Bose[2] stimulated anti-British demonstrations in Calcutta, despite having never been broadcast in India. The very objectivity of the English and foreign language services of the BBC can enrage special groups, even governments, who assume that the British embassy is in a position to control it.

The British Council has been even more the butt of satire than the Foreign Office, portrayed as purveyor of clog-dancing troupes, madrigals and Shakespeare readings to dotty expatriates and illiterate natives. Yet its major activity is mundane: in association with other educational agencies, it is the promotion of an annual migration of foreign students into Britain, and British students abroad. It administers the government's education aid programmes and various international cultural exchanges. It also supervises the teaching of English in its institutes and other colleges abroad. George Fisher is Council representative in Budapest:

Fisher:

We have twenty-two short-term visitors who come to Hungary from Britain; these are largely in the academic world. They cover a whole range of disciplines. We could have someone who's coming out here to look at Hungarian folk art, someone who's engaged on a learned thesis, a great many come out here for sociological and political research, but under the auspices of the cultural programme because they're academics. People also come out for technological

---

[1] An ATV drama documentary, broadcast on 9 April 1980.
[2] *The War of the Springing Tiger*, broadcast on 4 January 1984.

reasons: Hungary of course is a great drug-producing country, not of the heroin type, but of the medical type. Then there is the help that we give to Hungary, a great deal of it concerned with English language teaching. Britain can't be represented overseas politically and commercially alone. There has to be a third leg, and the third leg as far as I'm concerned is the cultural connection. The French have always insisted on this, on having a threefold representation overseas, and of course they have to pay for it. In every country I've worked there's been a very much larger cultural effort by the French than by the British.

What precisely these activities yield to British 'interests' is debatable, and much debated. The Think-Tank wanted the British Council abolished, with its aid work going to the aid ministry, education to the education ministry, and its overseas activities brought firmly under the Foreign Office's wing.[1] Much cultural representation abroad it found patronising and unnecessary, while the teaching of English, it said, should be a self-financing activity, run on business lines except in very special circumstances (as it now is). Where cultural relations were clearly an important part of diplomacy proper, for instance in communist states, they should be accorded full functional status within the embassy.

This is the rub. The British Council is an impressive organisation. Its 299 staff overseas, supplemented by 2255 locals, have a less restrictive lifestyle and more flexible career structure than the Foreign Office. While much of an embassy's work is inward-looking, cultural and educational relations are by their nature extrovert. The Council's libraries, cultural evenings and receptions are to an embassy's social fabric what coffee mornings and garden parties are to Tory constituencies. In contrast to much embassy entertainment, they bring 'non-Diplomatians' onto the premises and into contact with staff. Yet because all this is in the hands of a semi-independent body, it is regarded by diplomats as not quite diplomacy – as once they regarded commercial relations. The very independence of the British Council enables the Foreign Office to disregard much 'alternative diplomacy' and downplay its significance.

Proposals for expanding the role of embassies, however, are seldom greeted with enthusiasm in Whitehall. The issue of

---

[1] Op. cit. p. 223, para 12.76.

embassy size is almost as controversial as that of buildings. Britain is a full member of the international community and parliament and public show no desire to withdraw unilaterally. Indeed, MPs are often the most assiduous users of embassy services which they happily criticise on the floor of the House of Commons. Like grand opera, overseas diplomacy is a costly stage on which to play.

Our embassy in Budapest is probably typical of a medium-sized mission in a medium-important country. It comprises fifteen diplomats plus fifteen British support staff, mainly secretaries and guards, and another forty-six who are locally engaged. Behind the Iron Curtain more of these have to be UK-based for security reasons. Adrian Fortescue, head of chancery, regards this as about the right size:

Fortescue:

You can expect the British embassy to be somewhere in the second league in terms of size, behind the Americans but about level with the French or the Germans.[1] In terms of responding to London's demands we have sufficient trading opportunities and commercial opportunities to keep two people busy, the trend is upwards and therefore that seems to be paying off. Hungary is a country with an enormous cultural appetite, particularly in the field of literature, and within that field particularly English literature. So the availability of a library and opportunities to inform themselves about British culture and to learn the English language are opportunities which can keep two cultural attachés busy, and that's what we have. The consular side of life here is perhaps less busy than in some western countries, because there are far fewer tourists, although the Hungarians are starting up their tourist trade. As in any country, tourists can get into trouble, but we can cope with a part-time consul and a full-time vice-consul. On the chancery side, where we deal with political and economic reporting of developments in Hungary and relationships with other countries including our own, we manage with two people. I think one concentrating primarily on economic affairs and the other on political and press affairs is about right.

Embassies are visited regularly by inspectors who inquire into

---

[1] Diplomatic staff in Budapest embassies: UK 15; West Germany 11; France 14; USA 22; USSR 43.

each job and ask if it is strictly necessary. This process has cut staffing by twenty per cent since the 1960s. An embassy such as Rangoon had fifty UK-based staff when Nick Fenn was there in 1964. It now has seven: ambassador, head of chancery, commercial attaché (Burma is opening up to western trade), cultural representative from the British Council and three junior staff. It is hard to see how it could come down further and still be able to provide a normal range of embassy functions, with cover for staff on leave. Rangoon recently lost its defence attaché, to Nick Fenn's chagrin, as Burma is a military regime of the sort where doors might just open more readily to a soldier's uniform.

Successive reports on the Foreign Office have nonetheless suggested many posts could be reduced still further: to 'mini-missions' defined as three UK-based staff supplemented by local employees. One such mission is in Calcutta, once capital city of the Indian Empire, and still with a fine high commission building in a mansion near the Victoria Memorial, in which Britain's three surviving representatives now rattle about in lonely splendour. In charge is the deputy high commissioner, Tony Hayday, who describes modern diplomacy at its most skeletal:

Hayday:

In so far as there is a political interest, then you certainly need someone to keep an eye on that. That may not be a full-time operation but on the assumption that that job is done by the head of post then, by the mere fact that there is a post, he will have certain inescapable other functions to perform. So long as there is the potential for British exports, you would certainly need someone on the commercial side, and so long as there is a British community or a significant number of British visitors, then you would need someone on the consular side.

In Calcutta, the high commission may be minimal but Tony Hayday's residence is a point of reference for the British community and a help in time of need for Britons passing through. It is enough. The same goes for Britain's small and scattered missions in the Caribbean and Central America. It is easier by far to sense the shape of the embassy of the future in Calcutta or Rangoon than it is when confronting the myriad cocktail parties and underemployed chanceries of British embassies in Western Europe.

Balancing the costs and benefits of the various functions of a modern embassy is no easy task. Diplomats used to regard the 'unquantifiability' of their work as a useful defence against Treasury axemen. Many now wish they could lay claim to some index of productivity to resist that same attrition on costs. An embassy is, after all, a management unit spending money to achieve certain objectives. Any observer of its work is immediately struck by the archaism of its administration. The accounting methods and financial discretion allowed a head of chancery, even an ambassador, are less than that of a retail chain branch manager. Despite recent reforms intended to give embassies wider freedom within fixed budgets, a decision on whether to rebuild a waiting-room, hire a part-time secretary or invest in a word processor must all be referred to London. Office equipment is antiquated. Few embassies have micro-computers. Research and other support for even the most senior diplomats is minimal. Nor do embassies operate to annual – or even periodic – objectives against which their staff might be able to relate individual or collective performance. Their work is almost entirely reactive. Embassy size thus tends to reflect the size of its host country, rather than a specific task requiring to be done. It is essentially a Whitehall office system transported overseas, its dependence on London reinforced by the restless shuffling of staff between posts.

There are arguments in favour of such centralism. It ensures an embassy knows what London wants and does not go 'off the rails' without anyone noticing. It ensures co-ordination. At the same time, the style of management leaves little incentive for risk-taking or initiative by staff. Each diplomat knows that London is watching and pondering his next posting. This inculcates a conformity and an office discipline which is still remarkably reminiscent of an English prep school. Diplomats do not have any demonstrable measure of success. Marooned far from home, they naturally become obsessed with hierarchy, with their progress up the career ladder and with such intangibles as individual and collective morale. These problems are considered again below. We turn now to two missions so different they require a chapter to themselves.

The Twin Pillars

The Foreign Office is strict on one point of history: it never had responsibility for the British Empire. That was a matter for the India Office and colonial officials. The countries of the empire were kept in order by the rule of law and, if that failed, by the British army. The Foreign Office, divided until the 1930s into separate home and overseas services, dealt with the subtler art of dealing with foreign powers. It was an institution for negotiating, cajoling, plotting the national interest on the board of world affairs. The wielding of legal and military power was for colonial governors, soldiers, politicians. To a diplomat, to threaten was to have failed.

Nonetheless, from the 1850s to the close of the Second World War the might and wealth of empire conditioned each move in Britain's foreign policy. Empire meant an involvement in every corner of the globe and a reserved seat at every conference table. When it dissolved, Britain had to find new alliances to maintain her security and protect her economic interests. She found them in the North Atlantic alliance with America and in the Treaty of Rome with the European Common Market. These two relationships are the twin pillars on which Britain's post-war foreign policy has rested.

As such they tower over the modern Foreign Office. No policy is formulated or initiative undertaken without consultation with 'our American allies' or 'our European partners': third-world debt, the EEC budget, Middle East peace-keeping, sanctions against Russia, interest rates, nuclear disarmament talks. Missions in Brussels and Washington are thus quite different from normal embassies. Their work is more immediate, they tend to be busier, a constant flow of visitors from London tramps their corridors. Many of their staff are not diplomats at all but home civil servants on secondment. They have become overseas microcosms of Whitehall.

In a characterless block at the far end of Massachusetts Avenue's embassy row, 300 Britons and 200 Americans beaver away in the service of the British Crown. It is to a normal embassy what the National Theatre is to provincial rep. Here is the full works: social secretaries, press officers, attachés, consuls, communications experts, arms salesmen, diplomatic spear-carriers galore. The entrance is terrorist-proof. Combination locks guard each floor. There is a reception or party virtually every night somewhere within its premises.

Next door stands the famous residence, one of Edwin Lutyens' more coldly magnificent works. To inhabit it is the eminence of a diplomat's career. It is, however, the one Foreign Office nest in which that suspect cuckoo, the political appointee, makes a regular appearance. In the past fifteen years only one diplomat, Sir Peter Ramsbotham, has held the post in the normal course of his career, though a number have been appointed after retirement. One such is Sir Oliver Wright, who arrived to succeed Sir Nicholas Henderson in September 1982. To him, the Washington embassy is obviously special:

Wright:

Quite simply, it is the embassy to our friendly neighbour-hood superpower. It's a difference of scale. Other embassies are very important, but this one is qualitatively and quantitively different because simply everything that happens in this town is of importance to Britain and to the British government, and because we transact such a large amount of business here. Take, for example, the military relationship, that is the single largest component of this embassy. All four services, Navy, Army, Air Force, Marines, have a great deal to do with their American opposite numbers: the procurement executive is keeping in touch with weapons developments, defence sales are trying to sell some of our armaments to the United States. So there's simply a different scale, different order of magnitude of the business carried on.

And then there are the rows. Anglo-American relations are famous for arguments, some of them so fierce that they would tear apart friends less bonded by history and language:

Wright:

One of my very distinguished predecessors was having lunch with me the other day, and he said to me, 'Well, Oliver, how are things?' I said, 'Well, I've got five rows going with the Americans at the moment, one on extra-territoriality, one on unitary taxation, one on Pan-Am Services, one on Argentina, and one on subsidised agricultural exports.' He was here as ambassador to Eisenhower during the Suez days and he said, 'Sounds normal to me.'

If you're going to carry on rows of this nature which are of very considerable interest to Britain, to British firms and so on, you've simply got to have the people to transact them and try to effect a compromise which suits everybody's interest.

Transacting rows and effecting compromises is a good description of modern Anglo-American relations. Military and commercial links are so close as to require constant diplomatic lubrication. Less than 100 of the 300 British staff on Massachusetts Avenue are from the Foreign Office. The rest are from the Treasury, the Ministry of Defence, and departments such as Trade, Industry, Agriculture, Energy, Employment. This is not just a function of America's importance to Britain. The peculiar character of American government makes dealing with it a labour-intensive business. Power is diffused between the White House, Congress, the Pentagon and competing government departments and agencies. Robin Renwick, counsellor and head of chancery:

Renwick:

If you're dealing with an East European government, you're dealing with a monolithic point of contact. They will all sing the same song, you will get the story from everybody. If you're trying to operate with and on the American government to try to get your views across to them it is absolutely no use just going to the State Department. You have to go to the White House staff, the National Security Council staff certainly, the domestic staff quite possibly. You have to go to the Pentagon, you have to go to Congress which is a central aspect of the American government, and the process of lobbying Congress on all sorts of subjects is a major function here. If you are wise you have to make a real effort also with the American media who are virtually part of the American system of government and have enormous influence.

Two recent Anglo-American disagreements illustrate the strengths and weaknesses of British diplomacy in action. The first is the Grenada incident, the other is the long-running argument over the extra-territorial jurisdiction of American commercial law. Grenada was a disaster. Early on the morning of 25 October 1983, embassy staff were roused from their beds by communications officers informing them that the ally to which they were accredited had just invaded a Commonwealth country, without giving them any advance warning. The decision to invade Grenada had been taken by the National Security Council in total secrecy. Sources have disagreed over its reasons for not telling Britain: either it was assumed Mrs Thatcher would not agree or it was assumed she would. Either way, at the last minute the President spoke on the telephone to Mrs Thatcher direct. The terse conversation left neither side in doubt of her view. Mrs Thatcher, to whom the Grenada incident was a lasting source of humiliation, clearly felt let down by her diplomatic intelligence, both from Washington and from the Caribbean.

British diplomats prefer to dismiss the Grenada incident as quite exceptional. Yet it demonstrated starkly how an embassy can find itself cold-shouldered by the speed of modern crisis management and communications technology. It was neither in a position to predict a particular turn of events in its host country – the Americans shut even their own State Department out of the secret – nor was it a major actor in the subsequent foot-stamping. This was conducted by Mrs Thatcher in the House of Commons, and communicated by the news media instantly to the President's office. David Gergen was a special adviser in the White House at the time. The British embassy was simply not a factor:

Gergen:

If the President wants to have a message communicated, he will more frequently go straight to the Prime Minister. The degree of travel that has become customary in diplomacy also means that personal relationships develop between officials. For example, an assistant secretary for European affairs at our State Department will have friendships and relationships with individuals in the British government, in the Foreign Office back in London, so that they may just as well pick up the phone and call somebody in the Foreign Office as call the ambassador or someone in the embassy here. Now that's very different from the old days.

To Robin Renwick, however, the normal diplomatic niceties did not prevent emphatic messages being communicated:

Renwick:

The people we are in regular contact with were left in no doubt whatsoever of the strength of the irritation in Britain and of the difficulties caused by the inadequacy of consultation. The fact that several of those people are very close contacts of ours, people one sees a lot of, who in some cases certainly are personal friends, does not act as a handicap on you telling them how strongly you feel about something.

During the Grenada affair, Sir Oliver Wright was in a position an ambassador least enjoys. He was personally not averse to President Reagan's action, regarding it as a policing operation within America's sphere of interest. Nonetheless, over the previous few days he had been on the periphery of a decision process in London from which a view strongly hostile to American intervention had emerged. This he had to communicate to American officials, notably the Assistant Secretary of State, Larry Eagleburger. They in turn were unable to be frank with him, thus handicapping his ability to advise London. When the invasion occurred, he had both to maintain vigorously his Prime Minister's opposition to American policy and at the same time endeavour to repair relations and prevent them impeding the many other matters currently at issue between London and Washington:

Wright:

One is a shock transmitter and a shock absorber. To start with, under instructions, I had to make it very very clear indeed to the State Department that we hoped very much that the Americans would not take the action they did and give them the reasons why this was so. Then, when that action had been taken, I saw my task as really trying to steer the ship through the storm so that we came out on the other side rather more happily. And to some extent I think we've done this.

Grenada was a case of diplomacy having to sweep up a mess left for it by decisions of politicians operating above its head. The issue of extra-territoriality was different. It concerned Washington's insistence that American company law should govern the world-wide operation of British multinational firms as it does American ones. It erupted with particular virulence following Washington's imposition of sanctions against European firms involved in the Soviet gas pipeline contract. The issue was immensely complex, involving diplomats, businessmen and civil servants in London and Washington. The task for the embassy was to impress on the American government the strength of British feeling, with enough clout to get the policy changed. The impresario of extra-territoriality at the

Washington embassy was Rodric Braithwaite, minister[1] in charge of the commercial section:

Braithwaite:

There are cases going on in the American courts, arguments going on in the Congress, all the time, and British firms continually getting caught up in it. One really has to be monitoring all that, helping firms where possible, arguing with the Americans where necessary, as part of a continuous process. We have been very active here throughout the year in lobbying Congress and officials in the administration in connection with the new version of the bill to amend the Export Administration Act. This was the legal basis for the sanctions which they imposed last summer in the gas pipeline case and which they're trying to pass through the Congress at the moment. We want to get it better adapted to what we regarded as the realities of international life.

The subject had been raised a number of times at meetings between Mrs Thatcher and President Reagan, but it was an item buried at the foot of a long agenda, always remitted to junior ministers and officials for resolution. The issue required both considerable legal knowledge and a high level of negotiating skill. Negotiators must know their American commercial law – or at least enough to brief American lawyers to help them. They must be aware of the political pressures which the White House can bring to bear on the private sector through the Justice and Commerce departments. They must know the significance of the issue for British firms. It is not a job for the 'gifted amateur' – be he diplomat or politician – yet it illustrates the way in which home department experts, diplomats and ministers, interplay to produce the maximum negotiating effect.

Flying in a minister to conduct a particular set of negotiations is the Foreign Office equivalent of a tactical nuclear strike. It is only used as a last resort when all else has failed, and only with the most meticulous preparation and care. Even then, in a case such as this, the embassy might have been wary of fielding someone with a less sure mastery of the subject than Malcolm Rifkind, the responsible minister and a lawyer in his own right:

---

[1] A minister in the Foreign Office is usually a politician, but it is also a career grade of diplomat of junior ambassadorial rank, holding the number two post in a large embassy. To add to the confusion, there are three 'minister' posts in the Washington embassy.

Braithwaite:

So we started developing the idea between ourselves and our colleagues in London. Our aim was to get the Americans to field a high-level team of their own people in order to impress on them that this was a matter with all sorts of political consequences if we didn't manage it properly. In the run-up we explained to the Americans what we hoped would come out of the visit, so they would not be surprised by the sort of points that were put to them by Mr Rifkind, and so they would take the meeting seriously and field the right sort of people. We have told them often enough, and they know perfectly well, that this is a political issue, not just a legal one, and they accept that. But obviously having an elected politician coming out from Britain and saying to them in effect, 'You really should understand that the people of Britain do feel very strongly about this sort of thing,' is a rather more convincing thing to do. In the American sense it gets their attention, which is what we're after. Americans were also made to concentrate on issues because there was a meeting, they had to get together, produce their briefing papers and talk to one another. There is a co-ordination problem in Washington and various agencies don't always talk to one another unless there's a big event which forces them to.

A perfect negotiation is one at which there is no doubt on the facts of a position, no doubt on the terms of the argument and provisional agreement on minor points which officials feel confident will fall into place should the two or three major items be resolved. These items will be matters not of fact but of the relative strengths of political opinion. They should be susceptible to arm-twisting and horse-trading. Even then, officials will have gone over with ministers in advance what might be the implications of each concession. In this case the tactic worked. The Americans were induced to take the matter seriously and fielded the US deputy Secretary of State, Kenneth Dam, which in turn galvanised the State and Commerce departments into reviewing their positions. At a meeting[1] in Washington in

---

[1] The first fruit of these talks came in July 1984 when a bilateral agreement was reached on a procedure by which the US authorities may obtain access to documentary information in the Cayman Islands relating to offences connected with the traffic in drugs. It was hoped this would encourage equally successful outcomes to talks on other extra-territorial issues.

November 1983, it was agreed that talks at official level should take place on US attempts to apply their legislation with extra-territorial effect.

At any moment Whitehall will have a dozen issues such as extra-territoriality in contention in Washington. In the two months of October/November 1983, ten government ministers had passed through the embassy in the course of business, in addition to numerous official delegations, parties of MPs and others. The briefing rooms and dinner tables resounded to Grenada, Namibia, the Geneva arms talks, Nicaragua, trans-atlantic air fares, the sales chances for the Hawk fighter, the Lebanon civil war. For all such visitors, the embassy and the residence is base camp for the assault on the Everest of Washington politics. For example, a Foreign Office minister, Baroness Young, was in town for an exhausting series of meetings embracing arms sales to Argentina, Cyprus, Central America and the aftermath of Grenada. Good embassy briefing was essential:

Young:

It's very important, if you have just a half-hour to talk to someone, that you have made up your mind what it is you are going to cover, what it is you want to get out of it, and what are the real points that you must get across. Time is very limited, and it's well worth just going over the course to make sure you've got it quite clear in your mind and that you are not in fact repeating yourself to a number of people. So the briefing is essential. But it's a very well-oiled machine, the Washington embassy, and very efficient.

The machine's lubricator-in-chief is Lady Wright, the ambassador's wife. The paths of the two Foreign Office ministers, Janet Young and Malcolm Rifkind, crossed only once during the visit, at a dinner hosted by the Wrights. If the ambassador is master of ceremonies, his wife is producer and director:

Lady Wright:

The house, it's my tool of the trade. It's used extensively for entertaining. Lutyens designed it, it was opened in 1930, and he really did a superb job. The ballroom is used at the moment as a sitting-room with lovely couches and chairs. It can be emptied and we can also dance and really use it as a ballroom. Dinner parties: we can have thirty-two in the dining-room at a long table, and when it's all ready, with flowers, the glass and the silver, it looks very splendid. And you do see footmen going down on one knee to check that all the table napkins are in a precise row and all the glasses are in a row. The first time I saw it I thought it was very funny, but it's very necessary.

Visitors passing through Washington and privileged to have an invitation to the embassy receive immaculate attention. For Lady Wright and her domestic staff of twenty, it would involve:

Lady Wright:

Arranging dinner parties for them, seeing their bedrooms are comfortable and that all the stationery is ready and the flowers are in the room, seeing that the staff know when they're coming and when they're going to depart, so that they can look after their luggage. We've got a marvellous laundry service. Everybody can get their shirts washed and laundered in a day, which is very necessary when a minister is moving around the country. I reckon we run a four-star hotel, which is a full-time job, but I've got a very good staff. You couldn't work without a marvellous butler and a wonderful chef.

Such service outshines that of any Washington hotel or expense-account restaurant. And it is exploited to the full. Until recently, the embassy was criticised for dealing only with the White House and State Department and ignoring the pluralism of American government. It now accepts that Washington is a city of lobbyists and that the embassy is the lobbyist for Britain, no more and no less. It now has a section to 'sell' British interests to Congressional committees. It has another to handle arms sales to the Pentagon. Another deals direct with the Commerce department. Another tries to defuse the emotion surrounding the Ulster issue. For all these functions embassy hospitality is lobby-work of a high order. Sir Oliver Wright acknowledges its importance:

Wright:

Entertainment is one of the tools of the trade. Our houses are a part of that and one doesn't entertain simply to have a good scoff and a booze-up. One entertains because it does in fact facilitate the transaction of business. People are in a better temper when they know each other and have had a meal together.

The progress from drinks to formal dinner to coffee is planned and timed to enable a maximum of business to be conducted with a minimum of artificiality. Robin Renwick describes how that dinner party for Janet Young and Malcolm Rifkind was productive for him:

Renwick:

I found myself sitting between Ambassador Motley who is responsible for Central America, the Caribbean and Latin America, and Ray Seitz, the Head of Shultz's[1] office, who is an old friend. With Ray Seitz we talked about whether the Americans had an advance warning of the Israeli and French actions in Lebanon and what US intentions were there. With Ambassador Motley we talked about the US joint military exercises in Honduras and whether the Americans are going to send a contingent of national guards to Costa Rica. We also discussed Grenada and what the requirements would be after US troop withdrawal for help with the Grenadian police, and how quickly it would be possible to proceed to elections in Grenada. That's a matter for the governor-general and for the advisory council in Grenada, but it's a matter on which it's useful to know how the Americans see things.

But could such business not be equally well conducted on the telephone in the office – or at least over a modest lunch?

Renwick:

It is always possible to go to see these people in their offices and that is precisely what we do, but it is very much easier to get to see them in their offices and quickly if they know who you are. If they have met you and realise you know a certain amount about whatever it is, these people who are under very heavy pressure all the time will be less inclined to try and get people lower down to see you or to put it off altogether. Now the second point, and equally important in a town like this, is the fact that if you know the key people really well, you can then do a vast amount of business on the telephone with them. You can't do that if you're a voice out of the blue, who they don't know and aren't sure if they can trust. The socialising, the occasional opportunity to see them out of their offices helps in terms of access.

Away from the political arena, Roger Harding leads the embassy's defence sales operation. He is in no doubt of the techniques required for success in his part of the Washington jungle:

---

[1] George Shultz, US Secretary of State, 1982–

Harding:

Where any major piece of equipment is concerned, you've actually got to get the relevant service to want it, and that's very difficult. It means starting at the major and lieutenant-colonel level, making them aware of what Britain has to offer, and gradually working on through the chain of command. If the thing is in competition with an American company then there is a very real threat of lobbying from the Hill because of the Congressional interest in indigenous industry. So once you've approached the individual service and tried to convince them of the value of any particular product, the next stage is that they have to put it in a budget and that budget is then sent forward to the Department of Defense. The people there are concerned with the overall budget and generally speaking paring it down, so one has to have a number of contacts there to make sure the pet project of yours is not the one they cut out. It must then become part of the President's budget: so one tries to get to know the White House people, so that they can at least warn you if there's a danger of one of your programmes going. It then goes to Congress as part of the President's budget, and there it runs the same risks as any other American programme, but perhaps even greater risks if you don't have American support.

Why should the British arms industry benefit from such assiduous effort on the part of the embassy, at the taxpayers' expense? The answer is because that is the way Washington works:

Harding:

The American forces have very strict regulations about accepting hospitality from companies. This means that if you happen to represent a company and you ask a colonel for lunch, the chances are he'll say he can't come. But if the British embassy asks him to lunch there's no legal restriction on him accepting that.

Time and again at the Washington embassy, you will encounter officials neither looking nor sounding like diplomats. Roger Harding hails from the Ministry of Defence and has spent most of his career immersed in his present subject. Tom Harris is commercial counsellor under Rodric Braithwaite, on secondment from the Department of Trade and Industry. He joined in 1966 because he wanted a job which would take him abroad but without the constant shuffling of posts of a Foreign Office career. His only previous overseas posting was in Tokyo from 1969–71. He describes the difference he has noticed over the past fifteen years:

Harris:

In those days there was a certain sense of social and intellectual superiority in the Diplomatic Service. I think this has changed enormously. Here in Washington the atmosphere is really very different because this is a much larger embassy, where there's been a tradition of secondments from the home civil service going back to the Second World War. The mixture of representatives from half a dozen different government departments works extremely well. But I think there's also been a change in the Diplomatic Service itself. Its own perception of its role in the world and its relations with the rest of Whitehall have changed for the better.

There's been another change, too:

Harris:

So many of the diplomats that I'm working with have worked in positions in the Foreign Office which have brought them into regular day-to-day contact with other Whitehall departments. The head of chancery here was seconded to the European secretariat in the Cabinet Office when I was there, and we worked together very closely. The minister commercial here was the head of the European department in the Foreign Office when I was working on European affairs in the Board of Trade. So there is a shared experience that many of us have here whether we're from the Foreign Office or the Treasury or from the Department of Trade. We come from very similar backgrounds in terms of experience and dealing with similar sorts of problems.

Changed perceptions, certainly, but could it be that Harris is describing a very special sort of embassy – one in which non-diplomats are in the majority? Before coming to Washington full-time Harris worked on the aviation side of his department and was already continually flying over to keep in close contact with his Washington opposite numbers. Whether the Trade department needs an aviation man in Washington or can use 'visiting firemen' is a matter for that department. Diplomats do not come into it. The same goes for other specialist staff in Washington. Harry Walsh is economic counsellor on secondment from the Treasury. Or at least that is the formal position:

Walsh:

I'm dealing with technical economic subjects which normally diplomats, although they do discuss such things, don't go into in quite the same depth. I do it by relating what is happening in this country, and giving an assessment of the situation in this country. The formal position is that I'm on secondment to the Foreign and Commonwealth Office from the Treasury and therefore I report back through the ambassador on all issues. That makes the formal lines of communication quite clear. But of course there may be issues which the ambassador is not interested in and which the Treasury is interested in and in those subjects, largely of a technical nature, I report directly back to the Treasury.

For years the Foreign Office was criticised for failing to put across the government's case on Ulster, sending diplomats with plummy accents to defend the thesis that Ulster people really did want 'the British to stay'. Recently, in a fit of inspiration, the Office recruited Cyril Gray from the Northern Ireland Office. He is anything but a type-cast diplomat and has the advantage of a deep Ulster accent. He feels detached from the diplomatic side of the embassy, where officials lead different lifestyles and have a different set of shared experiences. He is also mystified how a career diplomat could have done his job effectively before:

Gray:

I find it quite remarkable the impact that an obvious Irish accent has on often very difficult Irish-American audiences. They may be many generations out from Ireland, they have a very imperfect, inaccurate knowledge of Ireland. Nonetheless, they do ask very detailed questions at all times and, to be frank, it's the only kind of detail you could know if you are yourself Irish and have been there.

These officials are doing work which is indistinguishable from that often considered the 'specialism' of career diplomats: negotiating and 'getting on' with foreigners. Yet it is precisely for their specialism that diplomacy has had to call them in. Here in Washington there is no room for the amateur learning on the job. The evanescent nature of presidential politics means that lobbyists derive their influence from longevity, from knowing the subject and the people round it more deeply than the next man. However brilliant a diplomat may be, it inevitably takes time to establish a close relationship with the professionals of the Washington circuit. Rodric Braithwaite, a generalist diplomat working in the specialist field of commerce, senses the limitation of the diplomat's career pattern:

Braithwaite:

There are so many people in Washington that one would like to know and that one needs to know. It's difficult to do it properly when people are here in the embassy for only an average of three years. One of the frustrations is that you get to know a large number of people very superficially, while it would be much better if you got to know a large number of people fairly well and a small group of important people extremely well, but that does require time. In this job I have to spread the butter much thinner than I've ever had to do in previous posts. It's a pretty slow process before one really gets on weekending terms with people, yet that's one of the measures of success. The test is whether when there's a row or trouble of some kind, you can ring up your friend and say, 'Look, we're in a fix, can't we sort it out without going through all those boring procedures?' I mean, that is the sort of relationship one wants to get on to with people, not whether you're on back-slapping terms with them as such.

Yet even Washington – that great factory of British diplomatic activity – remains an outpost as far as foreign policy formation is concerned. No matter how swift the Concorde flight or how active the telephone or telex machine, Massachusetts Avenue is 3000 miles from the centre of decision. Seen from home, it is merely one of many conduits of information, communication and advice in London's relations with Washington. Even a diplomat as senior as Derek Thomas, minister and number two in the embassy, is aware of being on the periphery:

Thomas:

Sometimes we are bold enough to volunteer advice to London on matters that we know to be under discussion. That's a prerogative of the ambassador in any post if he sees policies being put together in London which he thinks are going to affect either our bilateral relationships or our interests in the country in which he's posted, or which affect our relevant multilateral relationships, in this case NATO. I think that sometimes we do feel slightly out of touch with the policy-making process on a particular issue of that kind. This is one of the reasons why it's very important for the ambassador and some of his senior staff to get back to London quite frequently, to be in touch with the people who are involved in the sort of discussions which don't get put down on paper and transmitted out to embassies, in the way that they would perhaps be circulated round Whitehall. There are certain types of discussion in Whitehall which are never allowed to leave London, so that unless those of us who are here are able to go back quite frequently to London, in the Ambassador's case once a quarter, and in my case I try to get back once every six months, then we do risk getting slightly out of touch.

Washington remains, for all its idiosyncrasy, essentially a bilateral embassy, the supplier of a necessary service to Whitehall rather than an integral part of the foreign policy decision process. The second of our twin pillars, the UK delegation to the European Economic Community in Brussels, performs a different role. Here there is no host government to court and few representative functions to perform. Nor does the work involve the same cultivation of committees and cocktail parties of such multilateral missions as those to NATO, the OECD or United Nations. It is simply the steady grind of protecting British interests – often highly sectional ones – in the midst of an international bureaucracy which has gone increasingly haywire.

It is ironic that here in Brussels, far from the forms and protocols of bilateral diplomacy, the Foreign Office has found its strongest post-war commitment. On no political issue have diplomats been so outspokenly partisan as on Britain's membership of the EEC. They may be impartial to a fault on the trade unions or unilateralism or privatisation, yet they treat the 'European ideal' with a fervour which borders on the fanatical. From the early 1950s, this ideal responded to the diplomat's subconscious aspirations. It was untainted by the legacy of empire or the problems – and 'hardship posts' – of the third world. It was the theatre in which British diplomacy had been engaged since the dawn of political time. Now it had spawned an authority which reflected shared interests, unlike the abortive United Nations, and which was genuinely supranational. It would override the chauvinism and sectionalism of the home civil service. Sir Michael Butler, permanent representative to the European Communities:

Butler:

We are a European country and most members of the Foreign Office can see very clearly – if they didn't see before they joined then they see very clearly soon afterwards – that getting the Community to work properly, getting political co-operation to work properly, is vital to anybody who deals with the outside world in the second half of the twentieth century.

And were a young diplomat to step forward who felt that making the Common Market work was a less than vital matter – indeed that Britain should consider withdrawal?

Butler:

I think that their education on the subject of Britain's place in the world and Europe's place in the world might be a bit defective.

To David Hannay, under-secretary with special responsibility for EEC affairs at the Foreign Office, this commitment emerged with the new generation of diplomats who joined in the late fifties and early sixties, when Macmillan first applied to join the Community:

Hannay:

I don't think that there is anything particularly emotional about the Foreign Office's view of the Community, although it is often depicted as that. We are paid to advise ministers on what we think is the best way to protect and further British interests at a particular time. And I think a lot of Foreign Office people who have dealings with the Community have been deeply convinced that, with all its imperfections, it is the sensible way to protect our interests in particular sectors, that is to say the economic sector, the trade policy sector, and the foreign policy co-operation sector.

To the public, and to most home civil servants, the EEC is about economics: about trade and commerce, about farm support, about 'harmonisation'. To diplomats, it is also a crusade for wider political co-operation: the quest for the diplomats' holy grail of international security through alliances and the constant co-ordination of national policies. Europe is thus discussed by diplomats in terms seldom heard these days in Whitehall or Westminster. David Hannay again:

Hannay:

We believe that ten forming up in some capital of the world and saying 'This is our view' have more influence than ten separate people forming up and giving slightly nuanced different views. And if you're being shouted at and criticised by the people you're talking to in Ruritania or wherever, it's jolly nice if there are ten of you. As the Community is more important the other side doesn't tend to shout at you quite so much. They don't take on the group quite so easily as one of its individual member states. So, for a whole range of totally practical reasons, a lot of working diplomats see that this is an important way of developing British foreign policy in the latter part of the twentieth century.

It may be 'jolly nice' for diplomats, but does it matter? The limiting case of political co-operation was the Falklands war, when undoubtedly it did avert European division on an issue which could have damaged British interests. Swift work by officials under the then political director, Sir Julian Bullard, swung EEC governments behind Britain's position in the first week of the conflict. Community co-ordination was similarly achieved on issues such as the Soviet gas pipeline, on third-world debt and on Libyan diplomatic immunity. What difference such liaison made and how far it was dependent on the existence of specifically EEC political channels must be open to doubt. But the machinery was in place and worked.

The business of the European Economic Community is nonetheless chiefly about money. It is money which generates the bulk of the activity in the UK delegation's office opposite the vast and luxurious EEC Commission headquarters in the Berlaymont building in Brussels. It is money for British farmers; money from the social and environmental funds; money from Britain for the EEC budget, and vice versa. It is money gained or lost from harmonisation and deregulation, from import controls and protection, from changes in the relationship between Britain's economy and the rest of the world.

As such, almost every Whitehall department has a vested interest at stake. As Britain prepared to join the EEC in the early 1970s, a Whitehall battle was fought over how far it was to be a Foreign Office closed shop. The diplomats both lost and won this battle. European policy was to be co-ordinated at the centre in the Cabinet Office. This unit would always be under a home civil servant. However, the delegation in Brussels would

be led by a career diplomat. Such is the conservatism of Whitehall but this settlement has held ever since. Thus when the
Prime Minister and Foreign Secretary head off for a Euro-
summit, the co-ordination of their briefing takes place not in
the Foreign Office but in the Cabinet Office. It is here that
bargaining positions are hammered out into the night. As the
cameras click before negotiations begin, the delegation leader,
Sir Michael Butler, will be in the shadows behind Mrs Thatcher's
head. So too may be someone from the Foreign Office in
London, but there will also be officials from the Treasury, Agriculture or Trade. The king-pin is David Williamson, head of the
Cabinet Office European unit and a home civil servant who has
spent most of his career in the Ministry of Agriculture. To him,
the Foreign Office is just one of many departments with a
sectional input to the European briefing process:

Williamson:

It is the duty of the Foreign Office, in my opinion, to present
to the Foreign Secretary in the first instance and to the
government its view of what result should come out of a
particular discussion which is a) favourable to the UK, b)
negotiable, c) coherent with specific objectives. These are to
ensure that Britain's position in the world is presented and
maintained in the best possible way. But in the Cabinet
Office we are not Foreign Service personnel, we're not diplomats in that sense. Our job is simply to say, taking account
of the views of the Foreign Office about the negotiability of
this particular product, taking account of the views of
another department about the effect on British industry
directly, taking account of the costs in additional personnel
which appears on the Government's budget and all these
things, what is in our view the best result to recommend to
Ministers.

David Hannay does not diverge from this view, though he
describes the input a slightly different way:

Hannay:

On most of the technically complex matters the functional
departments – Agriculture, Trade, Treasury or whatever –
are undoubtedly going to make the biggest input into the
substance of our policy. They are going to write the basic
papers, and they are going to set out the facts and so on.
But there are an enormously complex number of tactical
choices about how to pursue that policy through the under-

growth, the rather lush undergrowth, of the Community institutions, and how to influence the other member states in their capitals on it. The Foreign Office input is often, on a case like that, with a high technical content, more about the tactics than the substance. But I think experience in dealing with the Community shows that the tactical choices are very very important, and if you get them wrong, if you just handle it in a very wooden way, you won't achieve what you're trying to achieve in Brussels.

Both Williamson and Hannay acknowledge that in European negotiating the essence of professional diplomacy is to present tactical advice for what will be a combat of specialists in whatever topic is under discussion. But even that advice requires detailed knowledge of the procedures and political techniques essential to the periodic EEC shoot-outs. Like Washington, Brussels is a one-game town. A personable sinologist out to broaden his world view will be beaten to the draw before he leaves the saloon. Sir Michael Butler knows this. Despite his Foreign Office background, he does not talk of the need for 'gifted amateurs' or for moving staff every few years to widen their horizons. Indeed, Sir Michael goes further and feels that the whole activity of Euro-diplomacy has galvanised the Foreign Office:

Butler:

It has given the Foreign Office still more to do. Certainly I believe that everybody works a lot harder now than they did when I first joined. I remember the other day I was walking down the Foreign Office corridor at ten to nine in the morning, and I met five of the six deputy secretaries all on different bits of business. Now, when I joined the Foreign Office in 1950 I don't believe there was ever a day on which you found a deputy secretary in the office at ten minutes to nine.

The European experience, in other words, like Washington, has confronted the Foreign Office with the need to conduct Britain's overseas relations 'at the coalface', with no time for genteel abstractions about career structure. Sir Michael has now been dealing with EEC matters exclusively for twelve years:

Butler:

Nobody ought to come to my job here without deep knowledge of the Community because there isn't time to learn on the job. In any case, if you came to be a permanent representative without having a deep knowledge of the Community, you might lose a number of very important tricks, which we can't afford to lose, in the first six months or a year that you are here. It's extremely important to know how the Community works, and to know the history of the subjects. Almost all these subjects have been negotiated on and off over a long period of time, and because there's a great deal of history to every negotiation you stub your toe if you run up against things which have been tried before, and haven't worked. All the people in the other delegations remember what happened before, and indeed other countries have a tendency to have people dealing with the Community for even longer at a time than we do.

Nonetheless, the nature of much of the delegation's work has drawn in large numbers of home civil servants. A quarter of the delegation are now non-diplomats, strongly reinforced from London, just forty-five minutes' flying-time away, during negotiations. Even for diplomatic staff, though many are loath to admit it, the EEC has become a specialism on which some may now spend the bulk of their careers. So integrated is the team that Sir Michael no longer detects any distinction between the professional background represented on his staff:

Butler:

I'd been dealing with the Community for seven and a half years in London before I came here, and I was surprised how little distinction there seemed to be in anybody's minds between the home civil servants and the diplomatic members of the team. Indeed, I never remember from one month to another who comes from the Foreign Office and who doesn't.

Yet to some of the diplomats working under him the Foreign Office interest in Brussels is more than just a matter of Hannay's 'tactical choices'. Emyr Jones-Parry is a rare Foreign Office physicist, whose current task in Brussels includes revising chapter six of the Euratom Treaty and the development of an EEC policy on coal. While other departments will be looking to sectional interests in these matters, he sees the diplomat as guarding a wider strategic view of Britain's national interest – what Sir Michael Butler calls 'ensuring the Common Market does not rot away by default':

Jones-Parry:

Coal policy clearly affects the Department of Energy, but to the extent that it impacts on the Community budget problem the Treasury would clearly have a major interest, so would the Foreign Office in terms of the development of the Community. The revision of Euratom covers, to a large extent, non-proliferation where the lead department in Whitehall is the Foreign Office. It's a merging of interest, it's not just one department. Now, why does it require a diplomat actually to achieve that? I think the answer is that it doesn't. It requires a particular type of skill. I hope that that skill is more likely to be found in a diplomat. He should have within his qualifications, his training, a packet of skills which particularly suit him to that.

And the definition of those skills?

Jones-Parry:

I think the major one would be to identify national interest, then to work out the best way of furthering that interest, to merge a technical knowledge with the political factors which are always inherent in any negotiation, and then to wrap it all up in a way which makes as convincing as possible an argument in favour of what you want. This should be in terms which don't necessarily link the UK with the desired objective, but in the context of the Community make it look an absolutely normal 'Communautaire' objective, one which should be inevitable and one which, if you advise it at the end of the day, you know is of great benefit to the UK, and one for which you pay as little as possible.

Thus identifying British interests with those of the EEC in order to win a point may be a deft negotiating ploy. It cuts little ice with hard-nosed home civil servants sent to Brussels to protect departmental interests against what they see as Foreign Office 'appeasement' of foreigners. Andrew Cahn is from the Ministry of Agriculture. He is formally on the Foreign Office payroll and is responsible to Sir Michael Butler as head of the delegation. But he is frank about his divided loyalty, as he wrestles to shore up the crumbling edifice of the Common Agricultural Policy on behalf of his client, the British farming lobby:

Cahn:

I think inevitably there have to be divisions of loyalty because one's future career is in the home department one comes from, and one is concentrating entirely on the subject matter of that department. This can manifest itself in particular issues. The Ministry of Agriculture which I have

91

worked for and will work for again would obviously tend to place great weight on the producer interest, that is on the farmers of Great Britain, because we are of course in constant touch with them. But the Foreign Office, when they are considering the same issues, will be more aware perhaps of financial constraints which the Treasury will feed into them, of the effects of relations with third countries who will want to protect their own producers, and on the broad national interest which will go wider than the simple agricultural producer interest. So one does find oneself caught a bit between two millstones. But this needn't be a problem. My present master is the Foreign Secretary, he pays me my income, he sends me my instructions, and I obey him, and of course there is a good co-ordinating machinery in London which makes sure that I get agreed instructions. Nevertheless I am in frequent, indeed constant, contact with the Ministry of Agriculture in London, direct. I talk to them more than I talk to the Foreign Office, and I think this is inevitable, because it is the Ministry of Agriculture which essentially does the negotiations on the Common Agricultural Policy, not the Foreign Office.

But what of the need to draw on the much-vaunted 'tactical negotiating skills' of professional diplomats?

Cahn:

I think that diplomats are in the business of getting the good will of their contacts, getting friendly with them, simply getting to know them, for some investment in the future. Here in Brussels we are negotiating on a daily basis about very large amounts of money, particularly in the agricultural sector. Therefore I think we tend to have less truck with rather fuzzy concepts such as negotiating capital, and rather more concern with the bottom line, how much money the UK wins or loses at the end of the negotiation. We do effectively negotiate agricultural policy in the Community and the result of this is that the Ministry of Agriculture has developed its own skills in negotiation and in a certain sort of diplomatic work. It now has rather less to learn from the Foreign Office than it did before we joined the Community. Indeed, there is some reversal to go through: I think the Foreign Office can now learn a few things from the Ministry of Agriculture about how to negotiate on the Common Agricultural Policy.

Indeed, the nature of diplomatic activity in Brussels is better seen as a constant struggle of interest: not just between nations but also between interests within each delegation. Andrew Cahn is negotiating the possible abolition of the 'beef variable premium'. His ministry wants it to continue. The Treasury is opposed on grounds of cost. The Foreign Office is inclined to agree with the Treasury. It wants reform, but nothing which might damage its baby, the EEC.

As in Washington, so in Brussels, this conflict of interest will be resolved not within the delegation on the spot, but at the Cabinet Office in London. Andrew Cahn and his colleagues will make their contribution through their various departments, but when negotiations commence in Brussels or through the summit machinery, an agreed view will be sent as an instruction from London. This process is acknowledged by all observers as a triumph of effective co-ordination. Yet even this co-ordination is seen as both a strength and a weakness. Peter Pooley, former Whitehall civil servant now at the Commission headquarters, is a constant recipient of British Euro-diplomacy:

Pooley:

On the whole I'm an admirer, not an extravagant admirer, of the British Foreign Office as compared with other diplomatic services that I see operating here and have seen in other parts of the world. They are very much amongst the most professional. A chap has a brief, and he has to keep within it. He has a system of instructions and reporting back which conditions the way he operates, and in that sense one can see that British diplomats, British civil servants in Brussels, because we have a very elaborate and efficient system of co-ordination in Whitehall, do tend to be tied rather firmly to their instructions and less flexible than some other nego- tiators here. The British have an obsession with consistency, which I think stems from the nature of our politics. Ministers must say the same as civil servants and civil servants the same as ministers. One department, say the Foreign Office, must say the same as another, the Department of Energy, and one must say roughly the same thing this month as one said last month, or have a good reason as to why one has changed. And so the British are more predictable. They are very well briefed, they are very articulate, it's very easy to get hold of and understand their point of view. It's relatively more difficult to change it.

This criticism of British negotiating technique is echoed, perhaps more obliquely, by David Williamson, who also worked at the Commission before taking up his present Cabinet Office job:

Williamson:

Our system is such that although we are very good at creating a position, sometimes we're, as it were, a bit too good at it. We overdo it, we go on perfecting our position and putting so many nuances in it that perhaps you do lose the thrust of what you're trying to do. You have to remember in the last resort that decisions in the European Community are not made by beautiful briefs, they are made by persuading people sitting round the table, most of them fed up and longing to go home, to feel that they've got to decide something which is usually not too pleasant for them, since we're usually presenting something which is advantageous for us. So you have to persuade people, and that is the underlying purpose of the whole operation. Sometimes I think that is lost a little bit in what I would call the meticulous and rather over-superb presentation of some of our cases.

In the competitive climate of Brussels, comparisons are inevitably made with other diplomatic cultures. Viscount Davignon is Commissioner for Industry at Berlaymont, and, like Pooley, a long observer of the British at work:

Davignon:

The French have, I would guess, a much greater degree of flexibility, not necessarily in terms of the objective, but in terms of how and when. I believe that in multilateral diplomacy, which is what we've got in the European Community, this is very important, because if you are negotiating with one person you know about what he has in mind after a little time, and you know about how things are moving. If you have ten people around a table, plus the European Commission, things are likely to go quite differently than what had been foreseen, because people are not going to say what one thinks they are going to say. They are not going to say what the British ambassador or counsellor thought that they would say after having asked Bonn or Paris, 'What will your people say in Brussels next week?' The first time the UK took over the chairmanship of the Council, it was not a great success because it had been

94

overprepared; not enough room had been left for the changes which occur because the mood changes, the people change, and you can't draft six months of multilateral diplomacy in advance. A lot of things will happen, some for good reasons, some for sometimes quite ridiculous reasons, but you have to take that on board.

Davignon traces British shortcomings back to the traditional relationship between ministers and officials, and the formalism this injects into their negotiating technique:

Davignon:

I would guess that the ministers in the other European countries, maybe because the administration and the officials are not as effective, are obliged to do more of their homework themselves. They are obliged to look at the problems themselves more and so come up with opinions of their own, and are more at ease with the detail. And it would be quite obvious that those ministers who opted to go into the detail themselves would be much more powerful negotiators in the Council of Ministers, or in any other forum of multilateral diplomacy, because they are on their own. I think the tradition built into the British system, of officials being separate and distinct from ministers, leaves less room for improvisation to reach the objective you want to obtain: improvisation meaning how you work it out, how you find room to accommodate the opinions of the others, making a genuine input at the actual moment of the negotiation. The preparatory stages are sometimes complicated by the detailed instructions which have been issued to the officials by other officials. The responsible ministers can feel in a certain sense protected by this enormous knowledge of their officials, feel that all the elements in the negotiation will be provided for them, as the discussion evolves. That can make them less agile to see an opening, or to use an opening, or to use the margin that everyone always has on a negotiation and to accept the concession which is needed to reach the agreement. That really has to be done by the person who is politically responsible.

The Foreign Office naturally does not accept this view of its performance. As far as it is concerned, co-ordination is the essential prerequisite for successful bargaining. The alignment of departmental interest, the 'squaring' of lobbies, the tactical briefing of other Brussels delegations, the consultation with embassies in the capitals of member states, all illustrate the smooth working of a good machine. One European foreign minister remarked that the British were as bad as the Russians: 'You meet two or three people in one day in different places and they all say the same thing.'

Of course, what to an opponent may seem inflexibility can be merely sound policy to a diplomat. Throughout the period of our inquiry, the British were adamant for a reform both of the Common Agricultural Policy and of the EEC budget system in general. True, this position reflected Britain's negative balance on its EEC account. But it is at least arguable that Britain's 'inflexibility' was right and, at the very least, was a ministerially-imposed policy objective, not a professional failing of British diplomats. The fact that throughout 1983 and early 1984 Britain was unable to convince its partners of its case might equally indicate a fundamental clash of principle which no amount of negotiation could resolve.

Yet even observers who were not unsympathetic to London's policy stance on the budget issue were infuriated by the manner in which it was sustained. This was not just Mrs Thatcher's personal style. It was what David Williamson termed (though not in reference to this case) a perfectionism in preparation and presentation coupled with an inability to react swiftly round the negotiating table. As a result, it is argued, Britain gained less than might have been on offer when a compromise of sorts was reached at Fontainebleau in June 1984.

In this chapter we have concentrated on Washington and Brussels because they are so unlike most bilateral missions, yet are also much closer to the popular conception of what diplomats are supposed to be doing. While many embassies seem intellectual backwaters, fussing over unimportant duties, these two are consumed by political activity. Bilateral diplomats describe their work in generalities about keeping in touch and maintaining good relations. Washington and Brussels diplomats talk in specifics: fixing this deal, squaring that opponent, protecting that interest. They work alongside home department officials and merge into the same lifestyle and work patterns. To the casual observer, all might be members of a unified civil service. Yet they are still abroad. As Derek Thomas said of Washington, they know they are executors of foreign policy, not its formulators. They seldom talk with senior British officials or ministers. They send more often than they receive. Rarely does their daily work have the exhilaration, or exhaustion, of political crisis management. Even when an explosion occurs on their patch, somehow the shock waves emanate from London. It is to London that we now turn.

Head Office

The Foreign Office is a daunting department. It is housed in an Italianate building, designed with a heavy heart by Sir Gilbert Scott in 1861 after Lord Palmerston had rejected his preferred Gothic. The result, overlooking Green Park between Downing Street and King Charles Street, is a sombre concoction of coloured stone and marble, its exterior decorated with panels portraying the extent and prosperity of pax Britannica. Inside, vast corridors, arches and sweeping stairways assure the visitor that here is omnipotence and omniscience.

All this can seem incongruous to a modern, post-imperial ministry of foreign affairs. The mismatch between architectural pretension and present function is a running theme of much outside comment on the Foreign Office: 'They still think they're running the Empire in there!' (which they never did). The department is not so much big as grandiose. Though numerically small, its scope is wide, both geographically and functionally. More than any other department, it works amid the reminders of its past, gazing down from portraits, spilling out of background files, emblazoned on the maps which paper its walls. For the Foreign Office, the past represents not so much faded glory as precedent, the raw material of diplomacy. Unavoidably it finds its way into the official subconscious.

The place has an aura of institutional assertiveness. A minister may jauntily enter with the expectation of grasping the tiller of foreign policy, obeyed at every turn by the most talented crew in Whitehall. He soon discovers that this is no ordinary department. The place and its policies seem to enjoy a symbiotic relationship. Altering the one involves changing the other; and changing the Foreign Office is something few ministers have been able to do in the short time they are usually assigned to its command.

Most incoming ministers have little experience of foreign affairs. As opposition spokesmen they may have read some papers and attended a few briefings. But the modern politician cuts his teeth on local government, industry or the social services, the subjects which concern constituents and win or lose elections. On appointment, junior ministers will spend much of their first year touring their geographical bailiwick – each minister takes roughly half a hemisphere. Abroad they will be learning all the time and meeting a baffling array of new faces. Except when embroiled in a crisis, they will be offered few chances to 'formulate policy'. Wise ones will either conform or risk being crushed by overwork and official obstruction.

The Foreign Secretary, Sir Geoffrey Howe, arrived in 1983 after four years across the road at the Treasury. How does he compare the two leading departments of state?

Howe:

Institutionally, at first sight, not all that different. The nature of the work is very different, because in the Treasury for the most part one is watching a series of dials, most of which move roughly in line with each other most of the time, although they occasionally get shocks from outside. In the Foreign Office one is looking at broad fields as it were, but they are much more likely to be disturbed by sudden eruptions, whether of a mole or a volcano. So it's a much less continuous life.

Sir Geoffrey finds the Foreign Office makes very different intellectual demands of its ministers:

Howe:

At the end of a long day, trying to study the latest Treasury paper comparing several different ways of measuring the monetary aggregate is actually more intellectually challenging than anything that emerges in the Foreign Office. On the other hand, the judgemental questions in both places are just as difficult, and I think that the Foreign Office is more likely to present sudden topics where you're required to absorb very quickly a great deal of information of a non-technical, but profoundly important, kind which is going to affect your judgement.

At the Foreign Office a minister must expect continually to be knocked sideways by unexpected circumstances. In most domestic departments, governments can pursue a semblance of a policy through from initiation to completion. A minister can claim with justice, 'I did that.' Any such ambition in foreign affairs is almost certain to be overruled by events. One junior minister, Nicholas Ridley,[1] entering the department in 1979,

---

[1] Nicholas Ridley, Minister of State, FCO, 1979–81; Financial Secretary to the Treasury, 1981–3; Secretary of State for Transport, 1983–

determined to make his mark by settling some long outstanding international dispute. He selected the Falklands, and it almost ended his political career. In most departments, luck plays a part in the public success or failure of a minister. At the Foreign Office, success is ninety per cent luck.

The textbooks state that the policy of a government is formulated in its manifesto, voted on by the electorate, approved by Cabinet, presented to parliament and implemented by officials. Foreign policy is different. International relations have to be continuous. Treaties and alliances must outlast governments and transcend partisan politics. The world balance of power cannot be adjusted overnight to suit the party in Downing Street. When one Foreign Secretary, George Brown, complained that the Foreign Office was resistant to policy change, he was told by Sir Cecil Parrott that, 'whatever politicians may say when they're in opposition, they soon find out when they get into office and read the confidential papers that they can't possibly do what they said they would do. They must instead follow the line of their predecessors in office, because there's just no other line any government can follow.'[1]

Diplomats thus experience a professional ambivalence not shared with other civil servants. They are certainly the loyal servants of the government of the day, yet they are also the custodians of continuity in British foreign affairs. Just as an ambassador is representative of the whole nation, so the Foreign Office official feels he is 'representative' of Britain's general overseas relations. He is not just outside party politics; he is above it. At times, this must inevitably set him against what a short-stay minister may require. Ministers also spend most, if not all, their time reacting to events. Even when they have a moment to play a part in some wider policy debate, promotion (or demotion) will usually carry them off before it is complete. Thus again it is officials who will seem to be leading rather than following in such a debate, with ministers as honoured onlookers. Malcolm Rifkind came to the Foreign Office as a junior minister after serving in a home department:

Rifkind:
A very high proportion of what one does on, say, housing or

---

[1] Sir Cecil Parrott, a diplomat 1939–60, first English translator of *The Good Soldier Svejk*, Professor Emeritus in Central and South-Eastern Studies, University of Lancaster, quoted in William Wallace, *Foreign Policy Process* (George Allen and Unwin, 1977), p. 52.

education or local government, stems directly, or indirectly, from the Conservative or Labour philosophy of the particular government that is in office. I think that is much less true when you are talking about foreign policy, where your actions are governed by the national interest of the country as a whole, which does not necessarily change simply because governments have changed. Most of foreign policy implementation does not consist of the dramatic initiative or the major event which you can initiate and then see brought to a successful conclusion within a fairly short period of time. That does very occasionally happen, but it's very much the exception. Most foreign policy consists of an infinite number of small steps and tactical decisions which may be part of a strategic policy initiative but which may take months or even years actually to come to fruition, even if it is successful. Therefore it is unlikely that you will be in office long enough to be both at the beginning and the end of a major strategic change.

Yet what are these long-term strategic changes over which individual ministers can have at best a marginal influence? The Foreign Office argues that since Britain abandoned a world role in the 1960s, the general lines of foreign policy have remained fixed. However much parties may argue in opposition about East-West relations or the future of Europe, no Cabinet has yet decided to take Britain out of NATO, abandon the British deterrent, end the Commonwealth or withdraw from the EEC. Britain has enjoyed a rough-and-ready foreign policy consensus. But does this mean that there is no role for day-to-day political input into Foreign Office decisions? Ted Rowlands was a Labour Foreign Office minister from 1976–9:

Rowlands:

I think that policy is a word that is much abused, and 'foreign policy' even more so than 'domestic policy'. The term 'foreign policy' implies that you have a largish degree of control of the situation and events that you're dealing with, whereas in fact there are always a number of elements which you can't control, and in many cases all you can do is react. What you try to do is to make sure that your reaction towards events does not conflict with the values and approaches and attitudes that you as minister and as a party believe in.

Rowlands recalls that when James Callaghan became Foreign

Secretary in 1974, he felt it would be a useful exercise to draw up a formal white paper setting out the intentions of the new government, supposedly for Cabinet approval and departmental execution. It proved abortive:

Rowlands:

It seemed a good idea at the time and we did all sorts of drafts. The problem was that by the time you'd omitted those bits we didn't want to tell people about, and those bits where we weren't sure what our profile was, you were left with about two paragraphs. We didn't bother to publish it.

Sir Geoffrey Howe set in hand a not dissimilar exercise when he arrived in 1983:

Howe:

One didn't come rushing in saying 'Here's a place that needs a great big shake-up because it's got a new boss'; I arrived as part of a continuous team. Even so, I did set in hand almost as soon as I got here a broad review of all the topics that were likely to be arising in the Foreign Office, some small ones, some long-term ones, some great big broad ones. The most obvious one was our handling of the relationship between East and West, where both the Prime Minister and I felt that one ought to try and see where that had been going wrong, if it had been going wrong; really, if you like, take it up by the roots and re-examine it.

Yet it is hard to detect any dramatic policy reorientation which resulted from this process. Officials explain that the reality of world events (reality is a favourite civil service word) naturally impedes any drastic policy change. The nature of the East-West balance of power imposes a framework which small nations such as Britain cannot hope to challenge. However much politicians may yearn for a positive foreign policy, they must ultimately listen to the voice of realism.

But who is to say? Are all aspects of British foreign policy imposed on us externally? Are none to be regarded as a matter of political discretion? And what of those areas where well-informed opinion is clearly divided? Foreign Office officials are remarkably unabashed over their commitment to their existing policies, to an extent which would make most home civil servants blush. Sir Antony Acland, as Permanent Under-Secretary, makes no bones over his department's response to certain well-canvassed ideas:

Acland:

I think that if a government were to decide to take Britain out of Europe, that would be very unsettling and worrying for a large number of members of the Foreign and Commonwealth Office, and I think for home civil servants as well. But there are other issues too which would cause them great anxiety: I think the withdrawal from NATO, or going wholly unilateralist, would also create great anxieties in the minds of quite a number of us. But I suppose in foreign affairs there has been a greater tradition of bipartisan policy over the years than on other issues, and it may have been comforting and consoling for us.

Sustaining this bipartisanship is a central article of faith to the Foreign Office. Consensus avoids public controversy and protects the continuity of international relations against the waywardness of politicians. Yet some ministers point out that this is merely another way of saying it protects the Foreign Office view against that of elected ministers. In 1974, a Labour government entered office with a policy from which officials strongly dissented, the renegotiation of the Treaty of Rome. Labour ministers heard the dissent loud and clear. David Owen was initially a junior minister, then Foreign Secretary:

Owen:

One became aware of the fact that quite unlike either the Ministry of Defence or the Department of Health, here was a very determined department which thought that its view was the right view. Now everybody thinks that, of course, but they seemed to want to carry on conducting foreign policy on the lines that they thought were right, irrespective of what ministers wanted. That did lead to quite a number of clashes. I didn't object to the clashes actually, I think ministers often make rather better judgements when they are challenged. I rather approve therefore of the fact that you could go to meetings and have a really strong argument. My problem with the Foreign Office was on implementation. Some officials, actually only a few but unfortunately once or twice in rather important positions, would fight the implementation of a decision taken by the Secretary of State.

How can a department so blatantly fight the publicly-declared decisions of its political masters?

Owen:

Well, of course briefing to the press is one of the most

effective ways that they do so. The most scurrilous briefing used to go on. It is actually very undermining of a position. If your European partners read in *The Economist*, or in *The Times* or the *Telegraph*, that there's a sort of unease about the position of the British government which is widely felt in Whitehall, they then begin to think, 'Well we can stand a bit firmer.' Sometimes you'd actually have it overtly said in your briefing material, that though this is likely to be said by the minister, his officials have briefed him in the opposite direction and they think you should do the following.

How do diplomats square these serious charges of bias with their professed impartiality and loyalty to ministers? Their answer is that they are simply pointing out to ministers the full consequences of what they are requesting. Foreign policy is a serious business with long-term implications. It is right that policy should go through a gruelling examination before being changed. Sir Michael Palliser, now retired, was Permanent Secretary during David Owen's term of office. What does he make of the Labour ministers' complaint?

> *Palliser*:
> I think it's understandable they should feel that way. Sometimes a very decisive minister is only really happy if he or she is having a fight. I'm not convinced myself that having to reach decisions by invariably having a battle is the best way of doing things because it imposes a certain degree of nervous tension on all concerned. But I would much rather have a decisive minister with whom I have to do battle occasionally, because he wants to do battle, than have an indecisive minister whom you feel would take your advice on almost anything, or who can't make his mind up. Frankly it is not the responsibility of the senior official to decide, it's for the minister. So give me decisive ministers and prime ministers any day of the week.

Yet there are times when even decisiveness is not sufficient to break obduracy. One of Ted Rowlands' areas of responsibility was Latin America, at a time of severe human rights violations in that continent. For diplomats, this is always a difficult matter: how to register governmental abhorrence of aspects of a host country's behaviour while still maintaining 'good relations'. In this case, the diplomats' instinct was clearly at variance with that of ministers. How did they register it?

Rowlands:

By actually putting up submissions and recommendations which counter those instincts. By saying, 'Don't you think we ought to perhaps bend a little in this respect or give a little?', or 'Don't you think that in the interests of trying to influence the events in Chile we might soften our attitude in this respect or that respect?' And the answer is no.

Ted Rowlands argues that Foreign Office officials simply refused to implement the wishes of ministers on what was, to them, a most important foreign policy issue, that of human rights:

Rowlands:

There's no doubt about that. If you have 135 posts or whatever it is abroad, the instinct of those 135 embassies or missions – it's quite a natural instinct actually, I don't condemn it – is to get on with the government they're trying to relate to, they would say, trying to influence. There were a number of times when I was in the Office, particularly because I dealt with Latin American issues, when in fact I said, 'No, we don't want to get on with that government.' Therefore the policy of that mission must be not necessarily to get on with them. Now that conflicts understandably with the natural instinct of the ambassador and his staff on the ground. It's a very painful thing to be told, 'Don't get on with someone.'

Not many politicians, even Labour ones, accuse the Foreign Office of overt political bias. Ted Rowlands believes that would be an over-simplification:

Rowlands:

I don't think it is a political bias. Class is the wrong word to use too. It's more to do with environmental background: generally speaking people from Merthyr Tydfil do not envisage becoming Her Majesty's ambassador in Paris. I think the bias is one of cultural perceptions rather than a straightforward Tory Party political or indeed a class-based bias.

Diplomats are well schooled to political impartiality and most are too shrewd to let that particular guard drop. Most traditionally vote Tory, nowadays some may be tempted by the Alliance, only a few will wink and admit to voting Labour – rather with an air of confessing to a brief night of sin. The bias, as indicated above, is not in party partisanship but in resisting risky policy innovations. Hence the aversion many diplomats feel towards Mrs Thatcher's brand of radical Toryism. Theirs is the politics of conservative pragmatism.

The institution in which this pragmatism is enshrined is divided into two broad areas of operation, one geographical, the other functional. The Foreign Office is a hierarchy of pyramids, of desk officers, heads of department, superintending under-secretaries, and overseeing deputy secretaries. The work of the geographical departments is straightforward. The Eastern European department has 'desks' (manned by first secretaries) for Hungary, Czechoslovakia, Poland and so on. Central Africa department embraces Zimbabwe, Zambia, Malawi, Angola, Mozambique and Zaïre among others. These desks and their departments are the 'head office' link for embassies abroad. Most departmental heads are of counsellor grade, yet they may have half a dozen ambassadors under their wing. Tessa Solesby is head of Central Africa:

Solesby:

Being a diplomat in London is much more like an ordinary civil servant's job. You are part of the Whitehall machine and you spend most of your time at your desk. There's a lot of drafting, submissions to ministers and briefing papers to prepare; you spend a lot of time consulting with other departments, a lot on the telephone, sometimes you go to co-ordination meetings. You spend quite a bit of time, though obviously much less, speaking to the public, British firms for example. You're concerned with the media. You have parliamentary questions to deal with like other ministries, letters from Members of Parliament and telephone calls from Members of Parliament to answer, so it is essentially a typical civil servant's headquarters job.

The plethora of instructions pouring out abroad from head office reinforces the sense of unimportance which can blight a modern mission. Tessa Solesby's account of this departmental supervision shows how far embassies have shed the 'plenipotentiality' of old:

Solesby:

The difference between what we do here in a department in London and what our posts do overseas is that the posts overseas execute policy on the basis of instructions from here, and they collect information which they channel to us, together with the recommendations for action. Our job, when we find these telegrams or letters from our posts lying on our desks, is to add information from other sources, to analyse and identify related issues, and to put the particular problem in a wider context, after consulting Whitehall. On the basis of all that, we then put up recommendations for action to ministers, normally in the form of a series of options. When ministers have decided, we then start the process again, and send off instructions to the posts to implement them. Certainly our job is not simply to pass the raw material which comes from a mission in the form of an ambassador's recommendations. Ministers will obviously attach a very great deal of attention to what an ambassador says, because he's the man on the spot. But an ambassador abroad cannot have the wider perspective which we have; he can't do the job that we do of connecting a problem with other problems, putting it in a wider context. He will be much less able even when it comes to tactics to decide, for example, whether the problem is better dealt with bilaterally or in collaboration with an ally, or better done through joint approaches through the ten members of the European Community. Also, of course, because we are a few doors away from our ministers, we do have a much more up-to-date feel of ministerial policy and the reasons behind it.

Nonetheless, every London-based officer is aware that his opposite number abroad may one day change places with him. He may regard him as an isolated unfortunate, but there is a natural relationship of sympathy. Morale must be upheld, and the natural inclination to send London more telegrams than it can digest is tolerated. This means that the production line for a Foreign Office decision can begin with a serious information overload from officers in the field. Edward Chaplin is Lebanon desk officer in the Near East and North Africa department, recently one of the Office's busiest sections. During the Beirut civil war, he watched a torrent of information pour across his desk from posts round the globe. What are his reasons for not reducing the flow?

Chaplin:

One is that you can't quite bear to give an instruction which would mean you get less information rather than more, because you might thereby miss that one vital piece of information you need. Second, I suppose there is a natural diffidence here in London to tell embassies that what they are reporting isn't wanted, because ninety-nine per cent of the time it is. It's very difficult to think of a neat solution to this. All you can do is have constant exhortations to people to be as concise as possible, and that certainly happens. Quite a useful innovation has recently been introduced, whereby people start off their long telegrams with a summary, so that sometimes you can get away with reading the first paragraph and forgetting the rest.

At the same time as material is coming in to the Foreign Office geographical departments from its missions abroad, a different information flow is entering through the conduit of the functional departments. These again fall into two categories. First are the essentially administrative sections, with little impact on foreign policy: personnel, training, security, communications, information, protocol, the inspectorate. Then there are what are colloquially termed 'marking' departments. These have developed rapidly in recent years to meet the growing specialism of much overseas work, liaising with and sometimes in rivalry with relevant home departments. The Foreign Office thus has within its walls a facsimile Whitehall, with 'departments' dealing with such subjects as defence, economic relations, trade, disarmament, nuclear energy, maritime affairs, aviation, the environment. These departments have proliferated as the Foreign Office seeks to maintain its interest in subjects of inter-departmental concern. If there is a meeting at Cabinet Office on the debt crisis, or the law of the sea, or East-West trade, or a joint energy project, it dare not allow the expertise of home civil servants to get the better of it. To other departments this can often appear as dangerous meddling: the Foreign Office defending the interest of foreign governments against the Whitehall consensus. Yet ministers and senior officials going in to bat daily against other departments see it differently. They feel the need of equal specialism 'from their own side' if a narrow chauvinism is not to triumph over a wider internationalist interpretation of British interests.

Len Appleyard is the head of one such 'marking' department, the economic relations department:

Appleyard:
The main role of the department is to act as an intermediary between the geographical departments inside the Foreign Office, and the Treasury, Bank of England and other departments outside. This involves knowing enough about the

technical issues dealt with by the Treasury and the Bank of England and other departments so as to be able to talk to them on equal terms, but also so as to feed in particular foreign policy aspects, partly by taking advice from our geographical departments – for example, on an IMF programme on a particular African country. There are political aspects to this which have to be taken into account as well as the normal IMF criteria. The role of my department is to make sure that these aspects are fed in accurately and that a balanced picture emerges. One tries to ensure that a decision taken in one part of the Whitehall machine does not, as it were by accident, have an effect upon relations in another area with a certain country. This is not because people, having thought about it, decided that this was a risk which had to be taken, but simply because they had never thought of it at all. You can't have that.

Many observers, inside and outside the Foreign Office, feel that this 'marking' activity has gone too far. Sir Robert Wade-Gery, now High Commissioner in India, previously headed the financial policy and aid department of the Foreign Office:

Wade-Gery:

I think we have too many functional departments. I would rather see the manpower that is in the functional departments redeployed to larger geographical departments. As I learnt when looking in from outside, what Whitehall departments go to the Foreign Office about is essentially expertise on 'abroad', that is to say expertise on France or India or a group of countries, the European Community or the United Nations. I was once put in charge of a department in the Foreign Office that was a kind of mini-Treasury and I thought it was a mistake. But I didn't stay long enough, I'm afraid, to do anything about it. It's a temptation to say, these home civil servants have got this expertise, we must learn a bit about it, and we must have a little squad of people who can mark them and follow what they are doing. I think it's a temptation one has to resist.

The goal of this welter of information and advice remains, in theory, ministers. Everything is written in their name and with their 'decision' in view. Yet most decisions are not classical enunciations of policy, the application of the mind of an elected politician to the facts and options for action presented to him by officials. They are messier than that. Most are urgent reactions to world events, catapulted upwards through the machine for presentation to a hastily summoned cabinet committee or meeting with the prime minister. The French have blocked lamb imports: how do we respond? The Turks are declaring independence on half of Cyprus: what do we do? The Americans are pulling out of Beirut: do we go or stay?

Such decisions cannot be contemplated in tranquillity. They are, as Sir Geoffrey Howe says, eruptions on the side of a volcano. The Foreign Secretary's private office is an operations centre, frantically channelling the streams of hot lava away from his desk while protecting his head from tumbling boulders. At any moment, his schedule may have to be wrecked while he flies off to Brussels or Hong Kong or drops everything to prepare for a Commons statement or debate. Sir Antony Acland describes the process from his part of the volcano:

Acland:
One consults a great deal. Of course one has to put up what one thinks is the best solution in a particular case, but it's not a rigid solution, and one doesn't do it without offering a whole lot of other options. Very often papers are put up to ministers saying, 'This is a very difficult question. There are four or five options, all of them fairly unattractive, and we think that on balance this one is the best.' You then have an office meeting to discuss it, you sit round the table and you say, 'This is a pretty nasty situation that we're in, and what is the least horrible of the various options?' There's no question of the Foreign Office putting up a tablet of stone, and saying to ministers, 'This is the only thing that you can do regardless.' It just doesn't work like that.

True, but there are subtle ways of ensuring that ministers come to regard the Office's preferred option as the best. To begin with, 'ministers' in practice usually means a meeting of officials chaired by a minister. As Ted Rowlands implied, any civil servant worth his salt will know how to steer a minister to a desired conclusion by careful briefing. Most decisions are anyway not matters of 'new policy'; they are judgements on the application of already existing policy to rapidly changing circumstances in which other departments will certainly have an interest. The question, as Sir Antony Acland says, is very rarely which option is best, but which is least horrible. And it takes a bold minister to demand a more horrible option than those already offered him.

The answer to the question 'What on earth do we do now?' will thus be based on a mixture of information, precedent and political common sense. Anyone present at a Foreign Office meeting, irrespective of status, should be able to contribute some, if not all, these inputs. Senior officials will normally feed in their experience of past policy – they are the 'memory bank' on which ministers have little option but to draw. This background experience will effectively determine what decision is feasible. As Sir Cecil Parrott said earlier, the closer you get to the point of decision, the fewer true options appear open. Baroness Young was the minister responsible for Cyprus at the time when the leader of the Turkish community there, Mr Rauf Denktas, declared UDI on his half of the island. How did the machine help her react?

Young:

Mr Denktas had been making noises about UDI for some time, certainly since last May [1983] when there was a UN debate on Cyprus. I went to Cyprus at the end of October, and said we would take a very serious view of that if he did. In spite of all this being said, he went ahead and declared UDI on 15 November, just about three weeks after I'd seen him. However, in a situation like that, where one suspects something may be about to happen, one does have an opportunity to consider all the alternatives in advance. We thought about what we would do if he did actually declare it, and consequently we were able to respond very rapidly. We got a motion down at the UN which was very largely drafted by us, we were able to encourage other countries not to recognise the North Cyprus Turkish state, we were able to get in touch immediately with the other powers, Greece and Turkey, who were guarantors with us of this Cyprus state under the Treaty of 1960. Now all these things had been talked about beforehand as possible lines of action. I never myself felt that if there was something else which I thought of overnight, or in the course of the day, something else which ought to be done, I couldn't feed it to the officials immediately.

When the crisis broke and the various 'possible lines of action' had to be undertaken, Baroness Young herself was not even present. Yet somehow they were discussed, selected and implemented.

Young:
When the actual declaration came, I was in fact in Central America. But everything comes in from the Foreign Office by telegram very rapidly and I was able to send back by telegram views that I had. I said that if it was really thought to be useful I would finish my tour off and come back. In fact it wasn't necessary, and there wasn't anything that I could have done, had I been at home.

Ministers' effectiveness in the decision process is severely limited by the Office's desire to have them out and travelling much of the time. There are good reasons for this: ministers gain access to their opposite numbers more easily and their presence raises the stakes in negotiations. But it inevitably means that decisions are often prepared in their absence, and at best all they can do is to race home to orchestrate presentation.

Many ministers can thus become no more than tactical advisers to the foreign policy machine, taking its tablets of stone and applying a rough political cosmetic to make them more acceptable. Yet selling a potentially unpopular decision can demand considerable skills:

Howe:
I think one of the things that people underestimate is the extent to which officials need political advice and steerance, the extent to which, much more often than not, officials are habituated and trained, whether they are in the Foreign Office or the Treasury, to say, 'Well, that's for ministers to decide.'

But in what sense do officials really defer to political advice and steerance? So often, it seems, the decision in foreign policy takes itself. What is left by officials for 'ministers to decide' is the manner of its passage through the political process, through Cabinet Office, Cabinet committee, to the House of Commons and on to the public stage. This is no formality. It is a question of how best to handle Cabinet colleagues, how to face a select committee, what to say at Commons' question time, what (if anything) to reveal to the press. The input of ministers to Foreign Office decisions is thus best regarded as simply the input of their own sphere of experience – politics. They are the impresarios of foreign policy. Even if history and world events supply much of the script, the success of the show will largely depend on them.

It is therefore strange that the most common criticism made

of the Foreign Office – by both ministers and diplomats themselves – is that its officials lack political sophistication, the one
quality ministers are supposed to contribute. The department
is regarded as aloof from Whitehall and out of touch with
Westminster. Diplomats may be kings of their embassies and
of the palazzo overlooking the park but they are innocents when
they stray into the jungle of interdepartmental committees or
the corridors of parliament. Malcolm Rifkind noticed this
immediately he arrived as junior minister and is in no doubt of
the reason:

Rifkind:

Foreign Office diplomats, unlike other civil servants, spend
a high proportion of their working lives abroad, and therefore are that much less aware of the political dimension back
home. But I think also that even during the period they are
in the UK they don't come into contact with the House of
Commons to the same extent that other civil servants do,
because there is very little Foreign Office legislation. In the
process of getting a bill through parliament, civil servants
attend standing committees, they sit in a box in the House
of Commons in the chamber, and they get a real feel for
what is possible and what is impossible in the parliamentary
process. Now clearly that is not something of which the
average diplomat would have much experience.

Certainly the links between the Foreign Office and parliament
are peculiarly weak. Foreign affairs debates and question times
are notorious for their poor attendance. Ted Rowlands recalls
his bleak parliamentary existence as a junior minister:

Rowlands:

The House of Commons doesn't actually debate foreign
policy very much. In my four years in office, I did about
three parliamentary questions out of fifteen, once a month.
I've got the world record for moving Southern Rhodesia
sanctions orders – five of them for an hour and a half at
some time in the middle of the evening – plus about half a
dozen statements regarding crises, and that was the sum
total of my parliamentary accountability over the whole four
years.

Much was expected from the new select committees set up in
the 1979 parliament. Yet that on foreign affairs has suffered
from weak membership, and its work has been consumed with
the overseas trips which are considered a major perk of com-

mittee service. It has yet to turn in a sustained critique of government foreign policy and is a pale shadow of its Congressional equivalent. It has not seriously troubled the Foreign Office.

The Foreign Office for its part has struggled to overcome both the criticism of its political naïvete and the problem of its distance from the political marketplace. Parliamentary liaison has been given a high priority. Sir Geoffrey Howe determinedly invites groups of MPs into the department for chats and briefing sessions. Further attempts are made to promote secondment and interchange of staff with home departments, to give diplomats more of a taste of domestic politics. Yet the gulf between diplomats and the rest of the political community remains wide, rooted in the former's exclusive career structure and the latter's treatment of the Foreign Office as a world apart.

To many observers, this distance has been reinforced by the steady drift of influence over foreign policy away from the Foreign Office towards the central co-ordinating arms of government, in No. 10 Downing Street and Cabinet Office. Officials draw a careful theoretical distinction between the 'formulation' of foreign policy, in the Foreign Office, and its 'co-ordination' with other departments, in Cabinet Office. The problem is that in the practical world of decisions, the international ramifications of domestic policy and the domestic implications of foreign policy both give an inevitable primacy to the co-ordinating function. In other words, it is what happens round the Cabinet Office table which really matters. Already Cabinet Office is specifically charged with such jobs as briefing ministers for summits, handling Anglo-Irish relations under the London-Dublin accord, servicing the committees of ministers which come into being during crises (such as that on Anglo-Libyan relations in July 1984). It houses the government Joint Intelligence Committee, which has a complete geographical staff to co-ordinate the flow of intelligence information from the Foreign Office, secret agents, the Cheltenham communications centre and other monitoring points round the world. The JIC thus has a crucial influence over Cabinet decisions in crisis management. As we saw in the last chapter, the Cabinet Office European unit is also in control of all negotiations with the EEC.

This development has in part been a function of the growing internationalism of most government decisions. But it has also arisen from the resistance of many prime ministers to the Foreign Office as an institution. Successive occupants of

Downing Street have felt the need for independent advice. This is not in itself a new development. Most prime ministers have liked on occasions to be their own foreign secretaries – Chamberlain, Churchill, Macmillan were all notorious for circumventing and abusing the Foreign Office when it suited them. George Brown, as Foreign Secretary, was particularly resentful of Harold Wilson's 'kitchen cabinet' and his appointment of non-diplomat envoys to perform diplomatic tasks for him, for instance sending Harold Walker to Vietnam and Lord Goodman and Sir Max Aitken to Rhodesia.

However, few prime ministers have been as vehement in their private attacks on the Foreign Office as Mrs Thatcher. From her early experience of Common Market negotiations – when she was convinced the Foreign Office was conspiring behind her back – through to the Falklands débâcle, she viewed the department with suspicion and regarded its ministers as tainted. Only Lord Carrington's skill and her own inexperience prevented many public explosions prior to the Falklands war. After it, she let it be known that she wanted a personal foreign policy adviser alongside her at No. 10. It was widely seen as an omen of the national security advisers of the American presidency, cause of such friction with the State Department.

The adviser she chose was Sir Anthony Parsons, formerly ambassador to the United Nations, whose straightforward language and lack of smoothness had so appealed to her during the Falklands crisis. Sir Anthony explains the need to which he was a response:

Parsons:

I think that if I were Prime Minister I would feel a slight vulnerability. I would feel that I needed to be sure that somebody on my behalf was constantly on the watch for crises suddenly blowing up, which would require me as Prime Minister to make very quick and very important decisions. I would feel more reassured if I had somebody alongside me who could give and would give a wholly independent personal view which I could match against the more formal advice which I was getting from the Foreign Office.

The appointment proved short-lived. In 1983 Sir Anthony was formally succeeded by Sir Percy Craddock, another diplomat, but Sir Percy was given special responsibility for the Hong Kong negotiations with a section under him at the Foreign Office. In the event, the Foreign Office had managed to resist this particular assault on its prerogatives. Sir Julian Bullard explains how Sir Anthony was carefully turned to good account:

Bullard:

Of course we set up a mechanism for ensuring that he knew exactly the lines on which we were working throughout, and we always knew pretty much the lines on which he was working. He was able to tell us, perhaps before we discovered it through our other channels, what were the Prime Minister's latest ideas and what were her priorities for the week we were in, and the week ahead. In the same way I think we were quite useful in letting Tony Parsons know the thinking of the Office before it crystallised to a point where we would want to put something on paper and send it across the road.

The Parsons appointment undoubtedly caused great consternation among diplomats at the time – much as does the periodic appointment of political ambassadors. The fact that it did not really work was a comment on how relatively immune British government still is to the rivalries and conflicts caused by the duplication of advice of the National Security Council and the State Department in Washington. For all the diffusion of foreign policy formation round Whitehall, the professional protocol that the Foreign Office is formal conduit for foreign policy advice to the Prime Minister has been maintained. Crucial to this protocol is undoubtedly the relationship between Prime Minister and Foreign Secretary personally. Many attributed the Parsons appointment to Mrs Thatcher's lack of confidence in her then Foreign Secretary, Mr Francis Pym. When Sir Geoffrey Howe took over in 1983, she no longer felt the same need for alternative advice. Sir Geoffrey had not only been practised in international affairs as Chancellor of the Exchequer, he had also established a close working relationship with Mrs Thatcher. Sir Geoffrey is clearly against any development which might drive a wedge between Downing Street and the Foreign Office in this way:

Howe:

I think it's important that the Prime Minister, with all the issues that cross her desk, whether it's foreign policy or tax policy or social policy, should have confidence in the officials by whom she is surrounded, who are necessarily few in number, who have to process this mass of information that reaches her, who have to advise her. I think that there's no great mystery in the way in which that's handled in our government. I myself would be pretty wary of the solution often canvassed for giving the government or giving the Prime Minister a free-standing set of advice somewhere else, somewhere out in outer space. You must face the problem of when is it going to make its input. Either it is just at the moment when the Foreign Secretary is formulating a proposition which he's going to discuss with the Prime Minister, and suddenly the boat is given a great shake and you start off all over again. Or it makes its input in the formative stage, in which case it will be no different from all the advice I get anyway. So I think there's a great deal too much tendency to look for institutional tricks to resolve the problem of securing a meeting of ministerial minds and taking decisions.

A similar relationship existed between Mr James Callaghan as Prime Minister and his Foreign Secretary, Dr David Owen:

Owen:

He had a remarkable gift for letting me know his views privately. He didn't have to send memos, he didn't have to write letters. Jim Callaghan could let you know just in a couple of sentences if he thought you were slightly going off the rails, or warn you about an attitude that he was going to adopt. Of course you're constantly in touch with the Prime Minister, perhaps more than almost any other minister, because you travel together a great deal. It's a crucial relationship. I don't think it's possible any longer to have a Foreign Secretary whose relationship with the Prime Minister is antagonistic or one of less than total trust. In the olden days you could have a Foreign Secretary who had an independent power base from the Prime Minister, and who held different views. But in the last twenty years that's become progressively harder to imagine. Inevitably heads of government are more and more being sucked into international affairs, they meet more frequently, they are involved in more detail, you can't shut the Prime Minister out any more. So the Foreign Secretary and the Prime Minister have got to have very similar views if the foreign policy of this country is to be properly pursued.

This closeness – both personal and political – between Prime Minister and Foreign Secretary is fundamental to the success of the Foreign Office, in retaining institutional influence over policy. We have traced the inevitable diffusion of power round Whitehall and to Cabinet Office as individual decisions of government demand more complex co-ordination. But the fact that the Foreign Secretary remains a senior figure in the country's political élite is the Foreign Office's greatest security.

A Future for Diplomacy?

The despatch box of the House of Commons is a wicked place to make a speech. There is no podium or arc lights or battery of microphones to distance a minister from his listeners. They pen him in on all sides, in front and behind. His opponents are alert and watching for any slip or hesitation. Even MPs from his own party will watch for signs of his having 'gone native' in his department. Many will covet his job. Hostility can be instant, vocal and unthinking. It is a good place for aggressive oratory; a bad one for the subtle allusions of diplomacy. Foreign Office ministers have traditionally had their worst moments at this despatch box. In recent years, on the Falklands, on Grenada, on Lebanon, on Europe, on Anglo-American relations, the meticulously calculated phraseology and soothing words have dried in the ministerial mouth. MPs on all sides have come to regard the Foreign Office as fair game for bullying, irrespective of which party is in power. It is not the minister they are after, but the department, almost the profession of diplomacy itself.

The unpopularity of the Foreign Office has naturally become a fixation with many diplomats, and has been noticed by many foreign observers. Viscount Davignon, of the EEC:

Davignon:

I have been in touch with British diplomats in a number of capacities for the best part of twenty-five years, and I have always believed that your Foreign Office is the best organised foreign service machine in the world. What has always bothered me has been, how such a good machine, with quite remarkable people, has a reputation which is not as high in some areas as the French or others would be. I have never found a very good answer to this. I am still asking myself the question.

Defenders of the Foreign Office argue that this failure to carry public conviction is due to its status as scapegoat for Britain's loss of world power. Politicians, press and public hold the Foreign Office responsible when its ministers have to bow to the pressures of world events they can no longer influence. The diplomat must be apologist for the reality of British impotence.

He is so often the messenger of bad news that some responsibility for it must rub off. His quandary is well described by Zbig Brzezinski, former President Carter's national security adviser:

Brzezinski:
What your diplomacy increasingly lacks is the necessary ingredient of power to back it. On the one hand that enhances the importance of diplomacy to the pursuit of your national objectives, since diplomacy becomes a compensation for your declining power. But your efforts to achieve some of your objectives are obviously made more difficult by the realisation that you do not have in all cases the power necessary to back up your diplomatic endeavours.

Yet the Scandinavians and the Swiss have developed a strong diplomatic tradition despite – perhaps because of – their neutrality and lack of military might. The French have turned self-interest into a most effective diplomatic weapon. Ironically, the most prominent events of British diplomacy in the past five years have involved the unfinished business of empire: the Rhodesian and Hong Kong settlements and the Falklands conflict. In each, Britain seemed able to turn adversity to good advantage without alienating potential supporters and with successful results. Olara Otunnu, the Ugandan delegate at the United Nations during this period, remarks admiringly on the operational techniques of Britain's diplomats:

Otunnu:
Some of the big powers, when they're in trouble and have a difficulty which needs to be taken care of, come on too strong. The reaction of the smaller countries is, of course, to become resentful, to become defensive and sometimes to be less than fully co-operative. I think the UK diplomats on the whole try not to throw their weight around too much. There was certainly evidence of this during the Falklands crisis when, even though Britain was directly involved, the weight of the UK wasn't being thrown around and that helped. And I suppose also there's always the British sense of humour which serves as lubricant in a situation, which was also on hand in the Falklands crisis.

Sir Anthony Parsons' winning of the Falklands vote[1] at the UN

---

[1] The vote was ten to four with one abstention. For the story of the vote, see *The Battle for the Falklands* by Max Hastings and Simon Jenkins (Michael Joseph, 1983), pp. 99–101.

Security Council in April 1982 is recalled by diplomats with the sort of awe normally reserved for a Jack Hobbs double century. Yet Rhodesia, Hong Kong and the Falklands were backward-looking incidents. To the former Foreign Secretary, Dr David Owen, the Rhodesian settlement in particular marked the end of an era, not the beginning of one:

Owen:

I often say that Lord Carrington was the last Foreign Secretary because it was a great challenge that both he and I faced, this last vestigial, major colonial responsibility. The whole world wanted to know Britain's view on what to do about Zimbabwe. It's hard to see an issue arising in which we will again have that degree of world attention focused on a particular decision of a British Foreign Secretary.

Certainly most of the foreign policy issues current during this study did not reflect well on Britain's independence of diplomatic manoeuvre. In the disarmament field, in détente and in the Lebanon, London seemed forced to respond to Washington's prompting. Over Europe, Britain appeared bad-tempered and ineffective, unable either to get its own way or accept a ready compromise. The one real triumph, the agreement with Peking over Hong Kong,[1] was yet another tying up of imperial business. Yet the political isolation and unpopularity of the Foreign Office cannot simply be ascribed to its policy predicament. There is – and to an extent has long been – a wider public suspicion of diplomats as a class. This Sir Antony Acland is ready to acknowledge:

Acland:

It is partly perhaps because we are known to spend a good deal of our time abroad. I think the slogan that we are 'the Office for foreigners' rather than 'the Foreign Office serving the national interest' is a slogan which has somewhat stuck. I don't think it's fair, and whenever I talk about the Diplomatic Service I say that we are interested in the formation of the national interest. In doing so you need to understand the position of foreigners, and the position of foreign

---

[1] *A Draft Agreement between the Government of the United Kingdom of Great Britain and Northern Ireland and the Government of the People's Republic of China on the future of Hong Kong* (HMSO, 26 September 1984).

countries and their likely reactions, but the starting point is the national interest. I hope that we can get that over.

Yet the very fact that diplomats seem to have lost a measure of public confidence in the conduct of foreign policy – and not just in Britain – indicates failures of professional structure and leadership which should be susceptible to cure. In this study we have observed British diplomacy from three angles: the diplomatic career, the institution of the overseas embassy, and the Foreign Office in London. For all our probing of its practitioners, we are left with a sense of diplomacy as still an elusive profession. It is an activity surrounded by abstractions, by myths which constantly obscure the issue of reform.

The first myth surrounds the diplomat's career. Virtually everyone we interviewed claimed that his (or her) specialism was in 'dealing with abroad': learning foreign languages, interpreting and reporting foreign politics, handling foreigners in representation and negotiation. Hence the hard language training, the learning on the job rather than formal induction, the constant shifting of postings and 'broadening of horizons', the entertainment and the cultivation of social graces. To Sir Antony Acland, 'Have diplomatic status, will travel' is still the essential denotation of the modern diplomat:

Acland:

It seems to me that you've got to have a group of people who are recruited under their terms of service to be prepared to go anywhere. When they get into the Diplomatic Service, they have to know and understand that the management are trying to take into account their personal circumstances, but that at the end of the day they have to be drafted to go to a post that they may not find, or think is going to be, particularly attractive.

Is this really true: and is it really the justification for an exclusive profession? As we have seen, there are now almost as many home-based officials serving abroad as there are diplomats. Most Britons working abroad use similar skills to those considered 'special' to diplomats: businessmen, journalists, aid administrators, academics. All must know how to deal with foreigners, how to learn languages, how to put down roots quickly in foreign countries – and pull them up again. What is more, their work increasingly demands of them skills which the generalist diplomat lacks. Sue Brown is an agricultural expert at the British embassy in Washington:

Brown:
I think mine is a specialist's job. Agriculture tends to be a very complex area, and it's helpful to have some background when one first arrives. Given the number of agencies in Washington, the extent of Congressional canvass, the lobbying organisations, which have to be covered when one first comes to Washington – in itself a formidable task – it helps if one has a basic understanding of the elements of agricultural support policies, both here and in the EEC.

These skills are increasingly crucial to the conduct of foreign relations. When challenged on this, diplomats argue that while twenty qualified people may have applied for Sue Brown's post, there is no such enthusiasm for jobs in less desirable parts of the world. Hand Washington over to non-diplomat specialists and able diplomats will be reluctant to be stuck with the dreary postings. Washington must beckon if Lagos is not to go begging.

We asked every home official we met whether he or she would accept what the Foreign Office calls a hardship posting. Almost all said yes, provided it was not for a lifetime. All they stipulated was that their particular skill be relevant to the job. Some had deliberately entered departments such as Trade or Overseas Development because of the opportunity of being posted abroad without the continuous dislocation of a Foreign Office career. Gerry Maguire, a Home Office official sent as immigration secretary to New Delhi, denied any problems in staffing tough posts:

Maguire:
We have substantial or significant numbers of staff in Islamabad, Bangladesh, Dacca, and of course Delhi, Bombay and Kingston. They are places where perhaps some people's first reaction might be that they were not particularly attractive postings. The lie is given to this because in the Home Office we have a system of advertising these jobs and there is no shortage whatsoever of applicants. The process is fairly competitive, in fact. We know that they are very popular because they are always oversubscribed.

Diplomats hold dear to the hardship posts argument because it is central to their conviction that their specialist skill, as against that of others, is in living abroad – a skill that is more difficult the harder the posting. Before the advent of cheap travel, student exchanges and hitching round the world, this might have been true. Living abroad has nowadays lost its mystery – and its 'specialism'. Yet the Foreign Office does not advertise most hardship vacancies, even round Whitehall, and must instead persuade often reluctant diplomats to do what they regard as penance, with the inducement of a more comfortable post in two years' time.

Equally curious is the myth that the Foreign Office practises fairness in the distribution of easy and hard postings, even within the top A-stream. In 1969 the Duncan Report recommended the Foreign Office should concentrate its ablest officials on an 'inner track' of London, Europe and America. The Office was naturally averse to anything which smacked of the old division between the London Foreign Office and the overseas Diplomatic Service, let alone the other class distinctions (such as with the consular services) supposedly ended by Sir Anthony Eden's 1943 white paper.[1] It would do no such thing. Derek Thomas, number two in Washington:

Thomas:

I don't think there's any sense in which we have two separate services. There was a recommendation in the Duncan Report in the late 1960s that we should have a sort of inner circle and an outer circle[2] and we rejected that, or the government of the day rejected it. The grounds were precisely that it would have a very bad effect on morale for there to be any feeling that there were certain people who were going to spend all their careers in comfortable posts and certain people who were going to spend their careers in uncomfortable posts.

Yet as we saw in chapter one, the 'fliers', the reserve fliers and the preferential treatment given to abler recruits, all suggest the Foreign Office does not practise what it preaches. The dissembling – for instance, fliers firmly declaring that their comfortable postings are 'really a lucky accident' – is far more demoralising to the rest of the Service. Others must indeed accept more than their fair share of hardship posts, and read the favoured careers of the lucky few in the annual Diplomatic List, known as the in-house 'stud-book'. Similarly, the old distinctions supposedly ended in the 1940s – such as the elevation of the consular service

---

[1] *Proposals for the Reform of the Foreign Service (Miscellaneous No. 2, 1943)* Cmnd 6420 (HMSO, 1943).
[2] *Report of the Review Committee on Overseas Representation* Cmnd 4107; Chairman: Sir Val Duncan (HMSO, 1969), p. 12, para 9.

to full equality of status – live on in the balance of E-streamers allotted to such work. Given the humble calibre of work done by many A-stream second and first secretaries, the class distinction between them and graduate entrants to the E-stream seems singularly unnecessary. It is hard for an outsider to understand why the Foreign Office still rejects a less stratified entry system, and a more openly meritocratic promotion structure.

We heard more grumbles on this score than on any other as we visited embassies, though professional cohesion means that Foreign Office grumbling is usually more in sorrow than in anger – often left to wives to express 'strictly off the record'. But there is a strong sense that less favoured staff are being overburdened as financial pressure forces cuts in establishment not matched by reductions in workload. Mike Jackson in Stockholm undoubtedly speaks for many journeyman diplomats outside the 'inner track':

Jackson:

I think almost without exception we are overworked, and things are getting worse. There are staff cuts every year. You seem to have the same or a growing amount of work done by less people and, because we are the sort of people that we are, signed on for the kind of career in the public service that we did, we try to cope with it.

One incidental aspect of these covert divisions is to lower the status of 'hardship' postings themselves – and thus of the diplomacy which goes with them. While the Foreign Office develops its cadres to deal with Europe and America – and to a lesser extent Russia, China and the Middle East – its attention to the third world inevitably seems more spasmodic. Posts are filled by a constant game of musical chairs, with little scope for the development of expertise. It is a discontinuity noted by Bill Luers, an American authority on Western foreign policy and now ambassador in Prague:

Luers:

In multilateral diplomacy there is a whole new culture that has evolved and the countries that do it best inevitably are the developing world. Mexico, Brazil and India, for example, are probably three of the most effective countries in multilateral diplomacy. They have a group of people who've developed over the years, know all the issues and attend all the meetings and are persuasive and conversant with past policy. That pays off in international diplomacy, especially in multilateral organisations.

Another myth of the diplomat's career is the importance of its 'roundedness': its generalism, its flexibility, its enabling a switch from commerce to Europe to information work to China – all at a moment's notice. It is presented as a necessary apprenticeship for the career's climax of ambassadorship. Such generalism is considered axiomatic by most diplomats to whom we talked – one even said he was a veritable 'specialist at generalism'. Axiomatic too is the process by which it is acquired. Sir Robert Wade-Gery in India:

Wade-Gery:

There's a constant tension that runs right through the profession. Every good head of post, every member of the public dealing with an embassy, wants people longer in posts. Most people who are sitting there doing the job want to stay longer in post. On the other hand, there is the requirement to broaden experience, and if you put somebody in one job for eight years, which has happened, you find that an awful hunk of his life has gone past and there are a lot of other things in other parts of the world that he hasn't done. Now that isn't a reason for whisking everybody around at a fantastic rate. But I can remember when I was involved as the secretary of the Duncan Report, we drew up a list of basic qualities which we said every ambassador ought to have had experience of in the course of his career. When we came to do our sums, we discovered that the man would have been sixty by the time he had that qualification, even on the basis of moving round much too fast.

To most non-diplomats, this is simply absurd. The work of British foreign policy should not be subordinated to perfecting the education of ambassadors. An increasing number of diplomats agree, resenting their Whitehall image as members of a generalists' closed shop and preferring to see themselves as simply civil servants working abroad. Rodric Braithwaite in Washington leads a mixed team of home and diplomatic officials, at the centre of which is a traditionally diplomatic skill – negotiating – which all share equally:

Braithwaite:

I don't see a very considerable distinction between diplomacy and what everybody in the civil service is doing. A lot of the time they are engaged in negotiating either with one another or with outside agencies of various kinds. I don't personally believe that negotiation is a particular mystery, and I certainly don't believe that it's something that only the Diplomatic Service has access to. We're all engaged in negotiating all the time. A lot of my home civil service colleagues in fact have more experience of negotiating with foreigners than I do for one reason or another, and they are very good at it.

This view of diplomats being challenged and even overtaken by home civil servants abroad is also noted by Peter Pooley in Brussels:

Pooley:

If one compares people as they come to you, very usually the home civil servant has had a good deal more experience of the Brussels scene by the time he arrives here in a representative capacity than the diplomat has done. So just on the basis of experience he is scoring. He also has rather more expertise in the subject-matter he is dealing with. Diplomats in Brussels are often running behind the home department, just trying to keep track of what's going on, trying to swot up the technicalities which are part of the everyday reference of the home civil servant.

The increased posting of home civil servants overseas, the secondment of diplomats to home departments for part of their careers, the diffusion of foreign policy formation across Whitehall are all steadily eroding the image of diplomacy as an élite and separate profession. Sir Robert Wade-Gery, who has seen more secondment to Whitehall than most of his colleagues, acknowledges this:

Wade-Gery:

I think one thing that people in the Foreign Office have learnt is to respect the expertise of home civil servants: the value of home civil servants from London dealing with a particular subject, talking to their opposite numbers in Paris or, for that matter, Delhi. Sometimes the moral for the member of the Diplomatic Service is that here is an expertise, some of which at any rate I need to acquire. I must know something about international financial affairs, something about international banking, whatever it is, something about civil aviation arrangements. Sometimes it is an awareness that the technicalities are so great that you need to judge the moment when you switch from trying to handle the problem yourself to whistling up somebody from London to come out and do it for you or alongside you.

Sir Antony Acland, ever ready to look on the bright side of change, interprets these developments not as challenging the diplomats' fortress, but as actually reinforcing the generalism which he so values:

Acland:

I think the consultation which now takes place in Whitehall ensures that British bureaucrats are more rounded perhaps than they were before, less limited, less specialised. The Foreign Office official understands better the agricultural problems, if he's dealing with the Common Agricultural Policy, or immigration problems, or whatever. This can only be beneficial. I also hope that through the interchange of ideas and the discussions that go on at Whitehall committees, the home civil servants understand rather better the perfectly legitimate foreign affairs implications of a domestic policy. That seems to be good for the national interest, and good for the individual civil servants.

Yet diplomats remain reluctant to carry this argument through to its logical conclusion: the integration of the home and overseas civil services. The idea has been about Whitehall for decades. To some it is simply an extension of the pre-war fusion of the Foreign Office and the Diplomatic Service. The Think-Tank report examined various options for recasting the Service, including its expansion to embrace the overseas divisions of all home departments. Recruits would enter a Foreign Service group which would include the Foreign Office and bits of home departments. The report marginally preferred such a solution, although aware it would signal the death-knell of the diplomat as a distinct profession.[1] David Owen does not agree with integration, but he feels that more cross-fertilisation than diplomats will tolerate is crucial to both home and foreign services:

Owen:

I think it would be quite sensible to have ambassadors appointed from the home civil service and have diplomats holding senior civil servant jobs. When Sir Donald Maitland[2]

---

[1] Op. cit. p. 355, para 21.54 and p. 360, para 21.71.
[2] Sir Donald Maitland, a career diplomat who joined the Foreign Office in 1947, was British Ambassador to the EEC 1975–9, deputy to the Permanent Secretary at the FCO 1979–80, and then became Permanent Secretary at the Department of Energy 1980–2.

was made permanent under-secretary of the Department of Energy I rejoiced. But I haven't seen a comparable senior home civil servant appointed to a major ambassadorship. If you could introduce cross-fertilisation at every level I think a lot of the problems of the Foreign Office would automatically be avoided, and I think that some much-needed internationalism and realism about the world would be injected into the home civil service. We made very concrete proposals in answer to the CPRS report about cross-fertilisation and I suspect one will find that none of them have happened – certainly not at the pace that was then envisaged.

A milder variant than full integration or even systematic cross-fertilisation has civil servants opting for availability for occasional overseas postings, with an understanding that this might include at least one hardship post. This would considerably widen the reservoir of officials for overseas postings and improve flexibility as a result. Either way, the changes overtaking diplomatic work and the strains at present imposed on individuals and their families are already fragmenting traditional career patterns (not just in the Foreign Office but in foreign services throughout the world). There is now a steady migration of diplomats in mid-career into home departments, and although the traffic is still one-way on a permanent basis, any dispassionate observer must regard greater integration of the two services as only a matter of time.

The diplomats' aversion to opening up their ranks to all Whitehall comers stems in part from the myths which surround their natural habitat, the embassy. Looking to America for clues to the future of British government is a dangerous game for reformers. But Washington's open bureaucracy reflects more accurately the changes modern politics forces on public service professionalism. There, the centre of influence and decision in foreign policy has drifted steadily away from the diplomats of the State Department and their embassies, towards the White House and its agencies. Zbig Brzezinski illustrates this drift:

Brzezinski:

I was many times in the Oval office when the President would reach for the telephone and phone up the Prime Minister of the United Kingdom or the Chancellor of Germany. The chances were that we probably wouldn't even bother to tell our ambassador that such a conversation took place because it was so frequent. That obviously has altered the role of the diplomat. I think we ought to have an inter-national convention updating the Congress of Vienna arrangements, streamlining and making more cost-efficient the activities of embassies – more like international business representatives abroad operate. This should take more advantage of computers and interface communications, outlining what the functions ought to be. Diplomats are no longer plenipotentiary negotiators. They are more social-political agents of influence. Emphasis ought to be placed more on these activities and more explicitly so.

British embassies rightly protest the importance of their work, but they cannot deny that technology has removed its traditional purpose, as plenipotentiary focus of one nation's political liaison with another. The Foreign Office pleads that national security must make it wary of the word processors, mainframes, facsimile transmitters and videophones of modern information technology. Yet diplomats with access to even the most modest equipment are aware of its implications. The European political co-operation desk at the Foreign Office is now in constant teleprinter contact with parallel desks in the foreign ministries of the EEC. This link, known as Coreu,[1] enables foreign policy liaison to take place instantly between officials, by-passing the embassies on the ground in European capitals. Tony Brenton, who handles Coreu, describes its operation:

Brenton:

It is an electronic means of more or less instant communi-cation between ten foreign ministries, completely by-passing the embassies, which formally are meant to be our means of communicating with the governments concerned. It is now within the bounds of technical possibility for me to sit here with a television set on my desk, able to look at and speak to, either separately or all together, all of my opposite numbers from the ten. It means I can get into contact more quickly with my opposite number in Paris than I can do with our embassy in Paris. I see more of him, know him better, and know his view on what French policy is going to be on a particular problem, rather better than I know what our Paris embassy's views on the same question might be. I think the bilateral embassy is already becoming a place which attends formal functions, engages in trade promotion,

---

[1] Correspondance Européenne.

but is increasingly out of major world problems. That doesn't mean that the bilateral embassy is going to disappear but it does mean that it is going to become part of the dignified end of foreign relations. What I would describe as the real business of actually solving problems and negotiating with foreigners is going increasingly to be done by experts and ministers travelling from their capitals.

In chapter two we examined many of the functions residual to modern embassies, concluding that they no longer really merited the ceremony and calibre of staff devoted to them. There is clearly a need in most countries for a British office, for consular services and for a political agent capable of supplying London, and visitors from London, with on-the-spot information and private hotel facilities. This function is put in a nutshell by Sir Robert Wade-Gery in Delhi:

Wade-Gery:

You may need people out from London who know a great deal about a particular subject. They are coming out basically to deal with their equivalents here who also know a great deal about the subject. But they need while they are here to work in partnership with people who know how to operate in Delhi. This is something to do with knowing people, knowing who is good, who's bad, who's effective, who's rising, who's falling, something to do with knowing local conditions, what you can trust, what you can't trust. So that the visitor from London can be reminded when he needs to be reminded that he's not dealing with an Englishman, he is dealing with an Indian. He mustn't find himself getting indignant when the man behaves differently from the way he'd behave if he was someone you met in Stoke-on-Trent. It's a partnership, and that partnership I would see as continuing.

This service is available nowadays to the whole of Whitehall. Indeed, many missions find the Foreign Office by no means the most important customer for their various services. Len Appleyard noted this when he was in Paris:

Appleyard:

People I had most contact with were the Treasury, the Department of Industry and the Bank of England. The Foreign Office came fourth on my list of departments with whom I had direct contact. I felt myself very much an arm of Whitehall and felt very closely in contact with the people in Whitehall. I didn't feel myself to be 'Foreign Office'.

Some of this agency work could certainly be subcontracted: neutrals such as the Swiss and the Swedes have made a minor industry of consular services in countries with which, for political reasons, major powers have no diplomatic dealings. Britain recently subcontracted consular services in both Argentina and Libya. The Foreign Office's information attaché network has already been much reduced though it still uses overqualified diplomats to perform routine inquiry work. One of the intentions of the Common Market was that collective EEC representation could supplant much of the work of embassies of member states. This economy has not been made.

British embassies, though no more lavishly staffed than those of comparable European countries, remain a 'high-quality' corner of the public service. Ministers, even MPs and journalists, are treated with an attention quite disproportionate to their importance – and certainly more than they would expect back home. We sat in on embassy discussions which debated at inordinate length the meetings, briefings, social engagements and cables to be sent back and forth to London on relatively insignificant visitors. Diplomats excuse this on the 'principle of infinite pains': that any visitor might one day be in a position to help (or worse, criticise) the particular embassy or the Foreign Office in general. Consulates have a terror of their customers writing to MPs. They quake at the prospect of questions in the House, which are all in a day's work to a home department. It is an insecurity fuelled by distance from London.

To some observers, however, the unimportance of much embassy work goes much further:

Brzezinski:

Diplomacy was once the national outreach to other countries, at a time when contact was difficult and contacts between societies were limited. Today diplomacy is no longer the exclusive outreach. It's one of many: international businessmen, journalists, academics and public political leaders. It really is quite absurd in this day and age of growing social austerity and social consciousness to have a small international trade union, which spends so much of its time – and the time of the spouses – entertaining each other under opulent conditions at the taxpayer's expense. It isn't really what their job ought to be about.

The cost and lavishness of representative diplomacy has always been a sensitive issue, if only because it is so hard to quantify the return. It is often reciprocal: there is not so much a return to entertaining as a possible cost to not entertaining. Undoubtedly in major world capitals, the custom of national day celebration – when each embassy holds open house for the others – is quite out of hand. One Middle East ambassador in Washington found he was expected to attend such celebrations two or three times a week or cause grave offence. He considered recruiting a double. Such representation is a severe, and often offensive, burden on the foreign exchange budgets of third-world nations. Most diplomats agree that too much food and drink is poured down the throats of other diplomats, but few are ready to stop. In many 'closed' countries, as we saw in chapter one, diplomats either socialise with each other or socialise with no one.

One subject on which British diplomats grow apoplectic is political appointments to ambassadorships as practised by Washington. Nothing has diminished the status of embassies in general – or been a symbol of that diminution – so much as the assumption that a major world power can be represented by contributors to party funds. Washington's active diplomacy is increasingly conducted by visiting officials from Washington. Local embassies – for instance, in the Middle East and Africa – are treated as little more than comfortable hotels, their staffs vainly seeking to exert some influence on a process taking place way above their heads. This is the more bruising to their egos when the visiting officials are themselves not career diplomats, but political appointees.

The Foreign Office has fought a long, largely successful war against any breach of its ambassadorial closed shop. Political appointments are occasionally made to Washington, Paris and the United Nations. Even then, the appointee has usually had some diplomatic experience. A controversial exception was James Callaghan's son-in-law, Peter Jay, who was sent to Washington in 1977. David Owen's enthusiasm suggests Machiavellian reasons for wanting his own man in such a job:

Owen:

I was greatly helped, to be quite blunt, by having somebody whom I totally trusted as ambassador in Washington. By putting a political ambassador into the circuit, I avoided having a complete network to which I had no access. The argument for having a political ambassador in either Paris or in Washington, or possibly both, is that no longer can the Foreign Office go on having a network of information from which the Foreign Secretary is excluded. You are plugged into the system, and I personally would strongly recommend any Foreign Secretary to do the same. It greatly helps to have a toe-hold in the bureaucracy through one of the key ambassadorships.

Although many diplomats regarded David Owen as merely cantankerous in this respect, he would argue he was more radical than most Foreign Secretaries, and therefore needed help in countering the department's conservatism. Certainly the appointment of ex-ministers and other senior public figures as ambassadors would establish closer Foreign Office links with domestic politics and public affairs than exist through the formal conduit of minister-at-the-despatch-box. To diplomats, whose whole career is a preparation for the job, this may be sacrilegious talk. But it might end the myth that 'rounded experience' is vital for ambassadorship. It might also mean less of the restless turnover of senior officials in London, as they vanish because 'their' embassy has suddenly become vacant.

Another advantage of the politically appointed ambassador is the opportunity it offers of bringing in new blood. Jeanne Kirkpatrick, American ambassador to the United Nations, is herself such an intruder:

Kirkpatrick:

I do believe the periodic introduction of different kinds of specialist – for example, the political scientist, which I am, or for that matter a politician legislator – gives some fresh perspectives, some new ideas. I think one of the pitfalls of very large bureaucracies is of a certain staleness developing, a certain lack of imagination, the tendency to the routinisation of everything. I think the introduction from time to time of new people at relatively high levels helps us fight against that. Unlike certain past ages when foreign affairs were largely diplomatic in character, and therefore reasonably left to diplomats, it has become a very different kind of activity in which diplomacy is only one tool. Foreign affairs today are multi-dimensional, including an economic dimension, a military dimension, and a cultural dimension with educational exchanges and communication functions and intelligence functions. There has to be a point in government which co-ordinates all of these perspectives on foreign affairs: it's very important to distinguish between foreign affairs and diplomacy.

But should this distinction be taken so far as to separate foreign policy and diplomacy into separate institutions, as in Washington between the White House National Security Council and the State Department? Back in London, as we saw in chapter four, Foreign Office diplomats have fought off challenges to their prerogative as purveyors of foreign policy advice to Downing Street, despite having been forced to concede some ground to the Cabinet Office. Yet the Foreign Office remains insecure in the world of politics, and is aware of the fact:

Acland:

It's a thing which worries me. I would like to see all our senior diplomats, indeed all members of the Service, brought home every year for leave, so that they can recharge their knowledge of what's going on in their own country. If you are a long way away from home, you do get out of touch. The political feel in Britain can change very rapidly, and you need to keep up to date with it. I'm very keen, and I think our ministers are very keen, on a greater interchange of ideas and thoughts and discussions with interested groups of members of parliament. I hope members of parliament whether from the government party, or on an all-party basis, can come into this building, perhaps under the aegis of a minister, to talk about a particular area, whether it's the Middle East, or the Caribbean, or arms control, or the United Nations, or whatever it is that interests them, so that we all get to know each other a bit better.

It is extraordinary that this proposal can still seem so novel to British diplomats. During the crises of 1982–4 – the Falklands, Grenada, the Lebanon, GCHQ and the EEC budget – many of them watched despairing as their policies were torn apart daily by parliament and the press. They longed to be able to rectify what they saw as the presentational failings of their ministers. British diplomats abroad are expected to be skilled at political manoeuvring and salesmanship. In Washington and Brussels, they must be practised lobbyists. Yet they nowadays have closer dealings with American congressmen and journalists than they are permitted to have – essentially by their political masters – back home in London. When they return, many are frustrated by this enforced isolation. Sir Nicholas Henderson has been ambassador in Bonn, Paris and Washington:

Henderson:

I have now retired finally from public service. In the last ten years of representing Britain abroad I have found myself frequently speaking, not simply to press conferences but also to the parliaments of the United States, France and Germany. I told them what Britain's view was on how Europe was evolving, what the Commonwealth was, what the Atlantic relationship was, and might become. But I have never, until after I retired, had a chance of discussing these subjects with, or even speaking to, groups of members of the British parliament. I've never been invited to. It was never expected that I should.

Certainly home civil servants play an increasing role in arguing policy with MPs, journalists and pressure groups. They defend the departmental line at public seminars and press conferences, accepting the risk to their independence which this implies. In the whirl of upheaving local government finance, privatising industry or reforming trade union law it is often not possible for outsiders – or insiders – to honour the genteel constitutional distance between official and minister so revered at the Foreign Office. Diplomats seem far removed from such a world. They rarely talk to the press, rarely go near parliament. They are like old family solicitors, guarding the paperwork and deferentially briefing the ministerial barrister when a crisis most carelessly occurs.

Sir Nicholas, like most of his colleagues, is adamant that nothing should be done which might interpose officials between ministers and the public or parliament. Others might be less constitutionally fastidious. However, even he is irked at the Foreign Office's refusal to use the material at its disposal to raise the level of public debate about foreign affairs:

Henderson:

I'm not trying to suggest that officials or diplomats should usurp the role of politicians and decide policy, or even persuade members of parliament that such and such a policy should be adopted. What I am quite sure about is that there's a great deal of factual material available in the Foreign Office that people collect all round the world, dealing with politics, diplomacy, commerce, finance, that is assembled by a few officials in the Foreign Office. This not only never sees the light of day but never reaches the eyes of those who, as members of parliament, are the ultimate deciders of our policy. Some system should be evolved by which all this mass of extremely interesting material should at least be available to those who have the responsibility for decision. In Sir Nicholas's view, considerations of security or international tact would require the censorship of only some ten per cent of such material. More radical reforms may be necessary to meet the Foreign Office's vulnerability to its critics not just in Parliament but in Whitehall. On this subject, Sir Robert Wade-Gery admits its sensitivity:

Wade-Gery:

The Foreign Office I think suffers from two things in Whitehall. One, it isn't there the whole time. People go and come, and you get people who come and work in the Foreign Office who haven't had the experience of life in the Whitehall jungle, which everyone else has. There is a lot of jungle craft involved in surviving, and not having it is a weakness. The other thing is that they suffer from foreign policy being or sounding rather airy-fairy. So many of the encounters in Whitehall that the Foreign Office is involved in are between a civil servant who is representing indirectly the interests of the steel industry, how many jobs, how much steel, something real and solid that people can understand and can measure, and somebody who is talking about British interests – the position we hold in the world, the danger that if we offend foreigners they may take it out on us in other ways. All this is much more amorphous and difficult to quantify.

That is how diplomats see the problem. To many home civil servants, the reality of decisions in matters of foreign policy has simply moved on from the days when it lay proud within the walls of Sir Gilbert Scott's palace. Increasingly it resides in the committee rooms of the Cabinet Office. It is here that officials fight out negotiating positions, brief ministers for summits, prepare the Prime Minister for foreign trips. David Williamson heads the European unit in the Cabinet Office:

Williamson:

A lot of the issues which are dealt with in connection with Europe are the responsibility in the last resort of a lot of departments: for example, how large should be a European programme on information technology, or research and development, or steel quotas. They are issues which in the old days would have been considered purely home matters. They now have this European Community dimension because decisions and discussions take place in Brussels. So it isn't quite the same as the old situation where you had some domestic issues and some foreign policy issues. We may have a clear position on some domestic issue but we have to present that position in a foreign policy context.

We saw in the last chapter that the Foreign Office's response to this diffusion of its traditional power has been to develop functional departments 'marking' the work being done elsewhere. Even if its control over decisions has weakened, it has sought to retain its influence over them as a major participant. David Owen shares Robert Wade-Gery's scepticism about this trend and argues that this arming of diplomats for interdepartmental warfare poses a threat to what should be the Foreign Office's constructive role in the future:

Owen:

It's a dangerous development because matching bureaucracy will never be able totally to hold its own and nor should it. It is, in effect, idle hands having to find work to do and I think they must not go down that route. You've got to develop close enough relations to be able to work with the grain of the home civil service – taking the best ideas and the best wisdom from wherever – and harness them to your international diplomacy. I think there is a great danger of the Foreign Office not being self-confident enough in its new role to operate very closely with Downing Street. If it resists that and thinks it can turn the clock back and have an independent existence, it will fail.

What all observers – from Zbig Brzezinski to Sir Geoffrey Howe – appear to be saying is that the influence of the foreign affairs bureaucracy in the future will lie not in maintaining an independent policy stance to be peddled to each new group of politicians sent it by the electorate, but in the opposite: in achieving a closeness to politics, to the Prime Minister and to Cabinet Office. We have heard a number of ministers reflect on the importance of the political links between them and the Prime Minister. The strength of the Foreign Office's position is also its institutional closeness to No. 10 Downing Street at moments of crisis or decision.

Sir Michael Palliser feels the Diplomatic Service should lose

no opportunity for contact with the Prime Minister as a means
of maintaining its influence on policy formation:

Palliser:

The British Prime Minister sees the German Chancellor bilaterally twice a year and the French President once a year,
and usually sees the other heads of government bilaterally
at fairly regular intervals. You've also got economic summits,
which involve the British Prime Minister and a number of
other heads of state and of government. It's inevitable not
just that a prime minister should be involved in foreign
policy because it's important but because he or she has now
to handle much more of it personally. This brings the Prime
Minister into much closer contact with senior Foreign Office
officials, indeed sometimes quite junior Foreign Office
officials. In my experience, whatever indignant sentiments
prime ministers may sometimes express about the Foreign
Office, exposure to good officials from the department
usually improves relations. The Prime Minister realises that
the officials are competent and the more he or she has a go
at them to make sure that that is the case, on the whole the
more they show that it is.

Not surprisingly, many now regard the Foreign Office's most
crucial 'ambassadorships' as not abroad at all: they are its
seconded (and usually its most able) officials at No. 10, the
Cabinet Office, the Treasury and the shifting structure of policy
units on the other side of Downing Street. For the Foreign
Office it is a case of 'if you can't beat 'em, join 'em'. It could
either slide into being another US State Department, a Whitehall
lobbyist for 'good relations with foreigners', its advice ignored
by a foreign policy machine which will sprout elsewhere in
Downing Street; or it must run with the political consensus,
even if it contradicts some of its own orthodoxies.

This brings the argument full circle. The task of overseas
representation still dominates the Foreign Service, encumbering
it with myths which tarnish its public image and cloud its
objectives. Embassy work needs to be clarified and set in context
and a more modest career structure evolved to match. The
élitism and esprit de corps from which diplomats believe they
derive their strength has paradoxically weakened them. It has
made them seem aloof and clannish. Whatever diplomats say,
they have resisted interpenetration with the home civil service
because they fear for their future as a distinct profession –

particularly their hold on ambassadorship. This fear is well
founded. Integration of the home and overseas civil services is
increasing daily. This is eroding the 'specialism' of the diplomatic profession and will continue to do so, to the point where
a separate entry and career structure will seem as unnecessary
as did the internal separation of the Foreign Office into home
and overseas before the war. The question is whether the Diplomatic Service will welcome such integration, or concede it only
under pressure of circumstance, harming its reputation in the
process. The diplomats' closed shop in international relations
is over. Every civil servant is now a diplomat.

Professional integration, as we have seen, should strengthen
rather than weaken the Foreign Office as an institution of
government by bringing it more in touch with the domestic
politics of Westminster and Whitehall. The case for an 'internationalist' input into government decisions is not just diplomats' special pleading. Where decisions have overseas implications, as an increasing number do, it remains important for
what is termed the 'Foreign Office view' of Britain's long-term
national interest to be expressed, even if it is sometimes overruled in the interdepartmental process. The risk for all foreign
affairs ministries – the domains of 'Diplomatia' – is that
professional alienation from political culture at home reduces
their effectiveness. They become just embassy-servicing departments. This is a risk of which many of those interviewed for
this study are aware. The reforms discussed in this chapter
cannot be dismissed as Sir Geoffrey Howe's 'mere institutional
tricks'. Since the Diplomatic Service vigorously and successfully
fought off the radical challenge of the Think-Tank in the late
1970s, many diplomats (not just the proverbial Young Turks)
have come to feel that more drastic changes in their Service
than those so far seen are now overdue. Many are enthusiasts
for more openness and resent the secrecy forced on them by
politicians nervous of their status and frightened of too much
public debate and scrutiny. Reformers of the Foreign Office will
find less opposition from within than is often supposed.

Who are these reformers to be? Government departments
perform as they do because that is the way elected government
wills it. Politicians do not like administrative reform. It is
difficult. Institutional resistance will always exist. It is politically
unglamorous and takes time to achieve fruition, let alone show
publicly tangible results. Ministers also have an instinctive belief

in their ability to put a personal stamp on policy, irrespective of the state of the bureaucracy. Only after they have failed do they blame civil service conservatism for their failure – and wish they had been bureaucratic reformers instead. The memoirs of politicians are filled with such remorse.

The fate of the Foreign Office thus lies not with Britain's diplomats but with Britain's politicians. The Foreign Office has a stock cliché for passing the buck when an unavoidably difficult decision has to be taken: 'Oh, that's for ministers to decide.' In this matter, they are absolutely right.

Index